Jewelry Flash
in a

Easy Earrings, Bracelets, & Necklaces in Under 1 Hour

From the publisher of *BeadStyle* magazine

KB
KALMBACH BOOKS

Contents

FAST
under 60
minutes
PAGE 9

Kalmbach Books
21027 Crossroads Circle
Waukesha, Wisconsin 53186
www.Kalmbach.com/Books

© 2009 Kalmbach Publishing Co.

All rights reserved. Except for brief
excerpts for review, this book may not
be reproduced in part or in whole by
electronic means or otherwise without
written permission of the publisher.

The jewelry designs in *Jewelry in a
Flash* are copyrighted. Please use
them for your education and personal
enjoyment only. They may not be
taught or sold without permission.

Published in 2009
13 12 11 10 09   1 2 3 4 5

Material previously published in
Under 1 Hour, a special issue
of *BeadStyle* magazine, and
BeadStyle magazine. *BeadStyle* is
registered as a trademark.

Manufactured in the
United States of America

ISBN: 978-0-87116-268-7

**Publisher's
Cataloging-In-Publication Data**
Jewelry in a flash : easy earrings,
bracelets, & necklaces in under
1 hour / from the publisher of
BeadStyle magazine.

   p. : col. ill. ; cm.

   Material previously published
in Under 1 hour, a special issue
of BeadStyle magazine, and
BeadStyle magazine.
   ISBN: 978-0-87116-268-7

1. Jewelry making--Handbooks,
manuals, etc. 2. Beadwork--
Handbooks, manuals, etc. I. Title:
BeadStyle Magazine.

TT212 .J494 2009

739.27

4 Introduction

5 Basics
A step-by-step
reference to key
jewelry-making
techniques used in
bead-stringing
projects

7 Beader's
Glossary
A visual guide to
beads, findings, and
tools

10 Elegance within reach A burst of
color looks radiant in a necklace and earrings

12 Big baubles, no troubles Necklace
and bracelet loom large

14 String a fabulous crystal set
Beading cones accent a crystal necklace,
bracelet, and earrings

16 Tie up a fast necklace Natural
materials make for down-to-earth fashion

18 The one and only Wire coils suspend
a single bead for one-of-a-kind style

20 Style at the touch of a button
Turquoise and gold unite in a quick
bracelet and lariat

22 Add personality with a floral focal
piece A nature-themed pendant
inspires a chain-and-crystal necklace

24 Briolette bangle Attach briolettes to a
bracelet form for a stylish bangle

26 Wear your hearts on your sleeve
Mix vintage hearts in a bracelet
and earrings

29 Do the twist Big beads make for a
snappy necklace, bracelet, and earrings

32 Zigzag dangles Showcase bright
beads on striking earrings

34 Breeze through a briolette
necklace A simple pattern makes short
work of stringing a two-strand necklace

36 Pearl-drops pendant Fashion a
simple and sophisticated custom dangle

2

FASTER
under 30 minutes
PAGE 39

FASTEST
under 15 minutes
PAGE 69

INTRODUCTION

It's about time. Feel like you don't have time to do the laundry, let alone take up a new hobby? You'll be surprised to find that this simple and rewarding pastime can be done in a flash. So take a few minutes for yourself, and explore!

You'll find many fashionable and stylish jewelry projects within the pages of *Jewelry in a Flash*, and they all can be completed in less than an hour. In fact, some will only take a few minutes.

Peruse the *Fast* projects in the first section of the book for under-an-hour beauties. Can you imagine a finishing a charming necklace and earring set like Lindsay Mikulsky's on page 22 so quickly? You can easily make it in an afternoon and wear it that evening.

Only thirty minutes to spare? Check the *Faster* section, full of projects you can complete as you watch your favorite sitcom, like Cari Rosen's chunky gemstone strand on page 52. Be done before it's time to tuck the kids into bed.

Is your schedule even tighter? Fifteen minutes is still plenty of time to make a project from the *Fastest* section, like Jane Konkel's bright and fun flower rings on page 82. You'll have everyone wondering, "Just how does she get it all done?"

Ready to get started? We've pulled all the essentials into the Basics and the Beader's Glossary sections. Step-by-step instructions make it easy to learn, even if you're new to beading. And detailed supply lists give you a ready-to-go shopping list to save even more time.

So switch your phone to "silent," toss the clothes in the washer, and set aside a few minutes for a simple and rewarding experience—creating beautiful jewelry.

A step-by-step reference to key jewelry-making techniques used in bead-stringing projects

CRIMPS

Flattened crimp

1 Hold the crimp using the tip of your chainnose pliers. Squeeze the pliers firmly to flatten the crimp.

2 Tug the wire to make sure the crimp has a solid grip. If the wire slides, repeat with a new crimp.

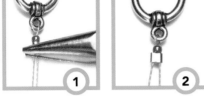

Folded crimp

1 Position the crimp bead in the notch closest to the crimping pliers' handle.

2 Separate the wires and firmly squeeze the crimp.

3 Move the crimp into the notch at the pliers' tip, and hold the crimp as shown. Squeeze the crimp bead, folding it in half at the indentation.

4 Test that the folded crimp is secure.

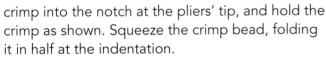

End crimp

1 Glue one end of the cord and place it in a crimp end. Use chainnose pliers to fold one side of the crimp end over the cord.

2 Repeat with the second side of the crimp end, and squeeze gently.

KNOTS

Surgeon's knot

Cross the right end over the left end, and go through the loop. Go through again. Pull the ends to tighten. Cross the left end over the right end, and go through once. Pull the ends to tighten.

Overhand knot

Make a loop and pass the working end through it. Pull the ends to tighten the knot.

Cutting flexible beading wire

Determine the finished length of your necklace. Add 6 in. (15cm), and cut a piece of beading wire to that length. (For a bracelet, add 5 in./13cm.)

LOOPS, JUMP RINGS, & WRAPS

Opening and closing a loop or jump ring

1 Hold the loop or jump ring with two pairs of chainnose pliers or chainnose and roundnose pliers, as shown.

2 To open the loop or jump ring, bring one pair of pliers toward you, and push the other pair away. String materials on the open loop or jump ring. Reverse the steps to close the open loop or jump ring.

Plain loop

1 Trim the wire or head pin ⅜ in. (1cm) above the top bead. Make a right-angle bend close to the bead.
2 Grab the wire's tip with roundnose pliers. The tip

of the wire should be flush with the pliers. Roll the wire to form a half circle. Release the wire.
3 Reposition the pliers in the loop and continue rolling.
4 The finished loop should form a centered circle above the bead.

Set of wraps above a top-drilled bead

1 Center a top-drilled bead on a 3-in. (7.6cm) piece of wire.
Bend each wire upward to form a squared-off "U" shape. Cross the wires into an "X" above the bead.

2 Using chainnose pliers, make a small bend in each wire so the ends form a right angle.
3 Wrap the horizontal wire around the vertical wire as in a wrapped loop. Trim the excess wrapping wire.

Wrapped loop

1 Make sure you have at least 1¼ in. (3.2cm) of wire above the bead. With the tip of your chainnose pliers, grasp the wire directly above the bead. Bend the wire (above the pliers) into a right angle.
2 Using round-nose pliers, position the jaws in the bend.

3 Bring the wire over the top jaw of the roundnose pliers.
4 Reposition the pliers' lower jaw snugly into the loop. Curve the wire downward around the bottom of the roundnose pliers. This is the first half of a wrapped loop.
5 Position the chainnose pliers' jaws across the loop.
6 Wrap the wire around the wire stem, covering the stem between the loop and the top bead. Trim the excess wire, and press the cut end close to the wraps with chainnose pliers.

Opening split rings

Slide the hooked tip of split-ring pliers between the two overlapping wires.

A visual guide to beads, findings, and tools

Glass and crystal

1 bicone crystal
2 round crystal
3 cube crystal
4 drop
5 briolette
6 saucer
7 rhinestone rondelle
8 glass flowers
9 seed beads
10 Venetian glass

Gemstones and pearls

11 lentil
12 rondelle
13 faceted rondelle
14 round
15 oval
16 rectangle
17 briolette
18 drop
19 chips
20 button
21 top drilled

Findings, spacers, and connectors

22 French hook ear wires
23 post earring finding
24 earring thread
25 magnetic clasp
26 lobster claw clasp
27 toggle clasp
28 box clasp
29 slide clasp
30 hook-and-eye clasp
31 snap clasp
32 crimp ends
33 crimp tube and round crimp bead
34 crimp covers

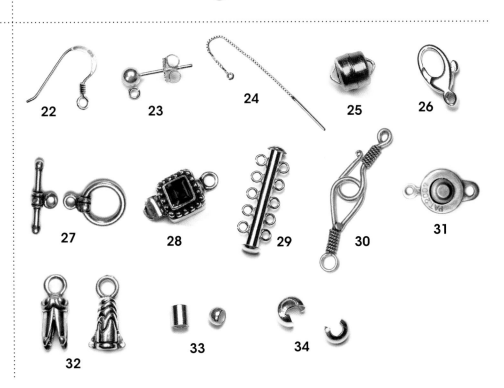

Findings, spacers, and connectors (cont.)

35 soldered jump ring and jump ring
36 split ring
37 spacers
38 bead caps
39 bail
40 cone
41 liquid silver
42 Wire Guardian

Tools and stringing materials

43 crimping pliers
44 chainnose pliers
45 roundnose pliers
46 split-ring pliers
47 diagonal wire cutters
48 heavy-duty wire cutters
49 ball peen hammer
50 bench block
51 ring mandrel
52 decorative head pin
53 eye pin
54 sterling silver wire
55 memory wire
56 flexible beading wire
57 leather cord
58 long-and-short chain
59 cable chain

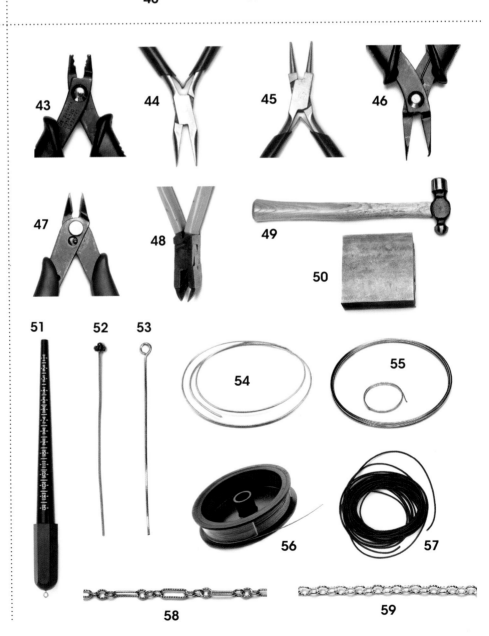

FAST

• under 60 minutes •

Instead of whiling away an hour, you can put together
a quick necklace, bracelet, or earrings. We used materials like
clay beads and colorful silk cord (page 16), shiny liquid silver beads
(page 10), and crystals in birthstone colors (page 14). And check out
a perennial favorite — a charm bracelet (page 26).

Elegance within reach

A burst of color looks radiant in a necklace and earrings

by Andrea Loss

Position a shapely assortment of crystals amid smooth liquid-silver beads. The contrasting textures and harmonious colors are a striking combination. You'll look impressive even when you're pressed for time.

1 necklace • Cut a piece of beading wire (Basics). (My necklace is 17 in./43cm.) Center a 4mm bicone crystal, a 15mm briolette, and a 4mm on the wire.

2 On each end, string: three liquid-silver beads, 3mm bicone, cube crystal, 3mm.

4 On each end, string: five liquid silvers, 3mm, bicone-drop crystal, 3mm.

Supply List

necklace
- 15mm crystal briolette
- 2 11mm crystal briolettes
- 2 6mm cube crystals, diagonally drilled
- 6 6mm bicone-drop crystals, top drilled
- 10 4mm bicone crystals, in two colors
- 20 3mm bicone crystals, in three colors
- 70–80 1 x 4mm liquid-silver beads
- flexible beading wire, .014 or .015
- 2 crimp beads
- snap clasp
- chainnose or crimping pliers
- diagonal wire cutters

earrings
- 2 15mm crystal briolettes
- 2 6mm cube crystals, diagonally drilled
- 2 4mm bicone crystals
- 14 in. (36cm) 24-gauge half-hard wire
- pair of earring wires
- chainnose and roundnose pliers
- diagonal wire cutters

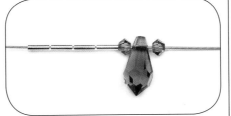

3 On each end, string: four liquid silvers, 3mm, 11mm briolette, 3mm.

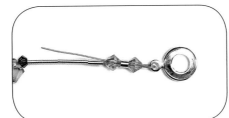

5a On each end, string five liquid silvers and a 4mm.

b Repeat steps 4 and 5a until the strand is within 3 in. (7.6cm) of the finished length.

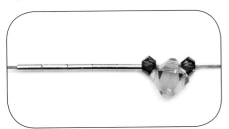

6 On each end, string 2 in. (5cm) of liquid silvers. String a 4mm, a crimp bead, a 4mm, and half of the clasp. Check the fit, and add or remove beads from each end if necessary. Go back through the beads just strung and tighten the wire. Crimp the crimp bead (Basics) and trim the excess wire.

WHERE TO SHOP
• All crystals and liquid-silver beads are available from Rings & Things, rings-things.com.
• Use 3mm bicone crystals that match the other crystals. I used three different colors.

1 earrings • Cut a 3-in. (7.6cm) piece of wire. String a briolette and make a set of wraps above it (Basics). Make a wrapped loop (Basics) above the wraps.

2 Cut a 2-in. (5cm) piece of wire. Make a plain loop (Basics) on one end. String a 4mm bicone crystal and make a plain loop perpendicular to the first loop. Repeat with a cube crystal.

3 Open a loop of the bicone unit (Basics) and attach the briolette unit. Close the loop. Open the remaining loop of the bicone unit and attach a loop of the cube unit.

4 Open the loop of an earring wire (Basics). Attach the dangle and close the loop. Make a second earring to match the first.

Big baubles, no troubles

Necklace and bracelet loom large

by Jane Konkel

Want a long look in no time? Incorporate earthy gemstones, a generous strand of wooden beads, and smaller faceted beads. Save even more time by stringing a short necklace — you'll need only a few sizable beads to make a prominent piece.

1 necklace • Cut a piece of beading wire (Basics). (My necklace is 44 in./1.1m.) String: spacer, rondelle, oval gemstone bead, rondelle, spacer. Center the beads on the wire.

2 On each end, string an alternating pattern of five wooden beads and four rondelles.

1 bracelet • Cut a piece of beading wire (Basics). String an oval gemstone bead, a rondelle, and a spacer.

3 On each end, string: spacer, rondelle, oval, rondelle, spacer. String an alternating pattern of ten wooden beads and nine rondelles.

Repeat the patterns in steps 2, and 3 until the necklace is within 2 in. (5cm) of the finished length.

4 On each end, string: spacer, rondelle, crimp bead, rondelle, half of the clasp. Check the fit, and add or remove beads if necessary. Go back through the last few beads strung and tighten the wire. Crimp the crimp bead (Basics) and trim the excess wire.

2 String a wooden bead and a rondelle. Repeat until the bracelet is within 2 in. (5cm) of the finished length. End with a wooden bead.

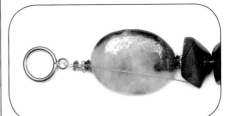

3 On the wooden-bead end, finish as in step 4 of the necklace. On the remaining end, string: rondelle, spacer, crimp bead, rondelle, half of the clasp. Check the fit, and add or remove beads from each end if necessary. Go back through the last few beads strung and tighten the wire. Crimp the crimp bead (Basics) and trim the excess wire.

Supply List

necklace

- 16-in. (41cm) strand oval gemstone beads, approximately 30 x 40mm
- **2** 16-in. (41cm) strands 15–20mm wooden beads (Rings & Things, rings-things.com)
- 16-in. (41cm) strand 5mm faceted rondelles
- **16–20** 6mm flat spacers
- flexible beading wire, .018 or .019
- **2** crimp beads
- toggle clasp
- chainnose or crimping pliers
- diagonal wire cutters

bracelet

- oval gemstone bead, approximately 30 x 40mm
- **9–13** 15–20mm wooden beads (Rings & Things, rings-things.com)
- **13–17** 5mm faceted rondelles
- **3** 6mm flat spacers
- flexible beading wire, .018 or .019
- **2** crimp beads
- toggle clasp
- chainnose or crimping pliers
- diagonal wire cutters

EDITOR'S TIP

The clasp enables you to double your necklace around your neck. If you intend to wear your necklace long, skip the clasp. On one end, string a crimp bead. String the other end in the opposite direction through the crimp bead, plus a few more beads. Tighten the wire and crimp the crimp bead.

String a fabulous crystal set

Beading cones accent a crystal necklace, bracelet, and earrings

by Stephanie Baker

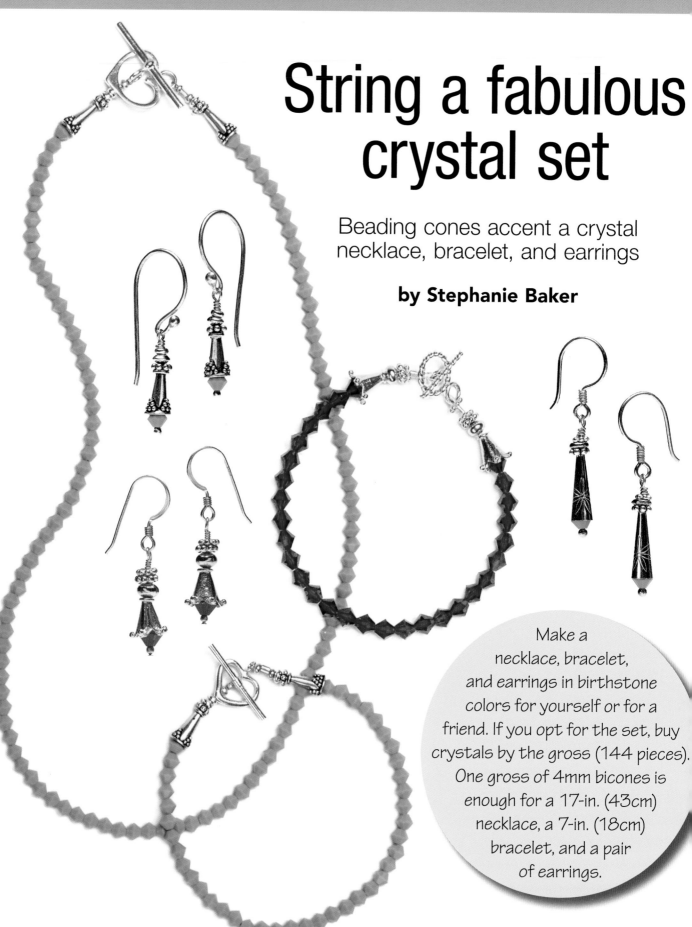

Make a necklace, bracelet, and earrings in birthstone colors for yourself or for a friend. If you opt for the set, buy crystals by the gross (144 pieces). One gross of 4mm bicones is enough for a 17-in. (43cm) necklace, a 7-in. (18cm) bracelet, and a pair of earrings.

BIRTHSTONES

If you like, use 5mm or 6mm bicone crystals.

 January: Garnet

 February: Amethyst

 March: Aquamarine

 April: Diamond

 May: Emerald

 June: Pearl

 July: Ruby

 August: Peridot

 September: Sapphire

 October: Opal

 November: Topaz

 December: Turquoise

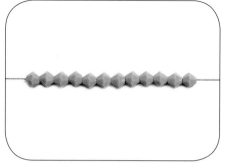

1 necklace • Cut a piece of beading wire (Basics). (My necklace is 17 in./43cm.) String bicone crystals until the strand is within 2 in. (5cm) of the finished length.

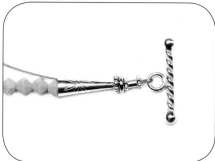

2 On each end, string: cone, two 4–6mm spacers, 3mm spacer, crimp bead, 3mm spacer, half of the clasp. Check the fit, and add or remove beads if necessary. Go back through the beads just strung and tighten the wire. Crimp the crimp beads (Basics) and trim the excess wire.

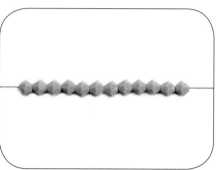

bracelet • Cut a piece of beading wire (Basics). String bicone crystals until the strand is within 2 in. (5cm) of the finished length. Finish as in step 2 of the necklace.

1 earrings • On a decorative head pin, string a bicone crystal, a cone, and three spacers. Make a wrapped loop (Basics).

2 Open the loop of an earring wire (Basics). Attach the dangle and close the loop. Make a second earring to match the first.

Supply List

necklace
- **100–130** 4mm bicone crystals
- **4** 4–6mm flat spacers
- **4** 3mm flat spacers
- flexible beading wire, .014 or .015
- 2 cones, with 3–4mm bottom opening
- 2 crimp beads
- toggle clasp
- chainnose or crimping pliers
- diagonal wire cutters

bracelet
- **35–45** 4mm bicone crystals
- **4** 4–6mm flat spacers
- **4** 3mm flat spacers
- flexible beading wire, .014 or .015
- 2 cones, with 3–4mm bottom opening
- 2 crimp beads
- toggle clasp
- chainnose or crimping pliers
- diagonal wire cutters

earrings
- **2** 4mm bicone crystals
- **6** 3–6mm flat spacers, in three styles
- **2** 2-in. (5cm) decorative head pins
- **2** cones, with 3–4mm bottom opening
- pair of earring wires
- chainnose and roundnose pliers
- diagonal wire cutters

Tie up a fast necklace

Natural materials make for down-to-earth fashion

by Lindsay Mikulsky

Multicolored clay beads and silk cord in a bold accent color create a substantial look that's great for everyday wear. Simple overhand knots and an easy finishing technique make this necklace a breeze to put together.

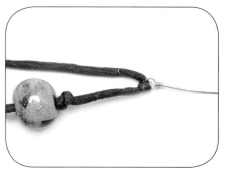

1 On a silk cord, string and center a large-hole bead. Tie an overhand knot (Basics) on each side of the bead.

2 On each end, string a bead and tie an overhand knot. Repeat until the necklace is within 2 in. (5cm) of the finished length. (My necklace is 14 in./36cm.)

3 Cut a 3-in. (7.6cm) piece of wire. Make a wrapped loop (Basics) on one end. Repeat.

On each end, 1 in. (2.5cm) from the last bead, tie an overhand knot on a wrapped loop. Trim the excess cord, and apply glue to the knot.

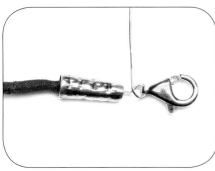

4 On each wire, string a cone. Make the first half of a wrapped loop. On one end, attach a lobster claw clasp. On the other end, attach a soldered jump ring. Complete the wraps.

EDITOR'S TIP

If you're having trouble stringing the beads, make a "needle" using .014 or .015 beading wire. Flatten a 1mm crimp tube to secure the eye of the needle.

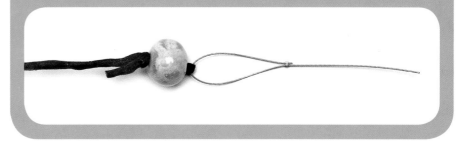

DESIGN OPTION

If you want to show more cord, leave a 1-in. (2.5cm) space between the beads.

Supply List

- **17–25** 12mm round large-hole beads (glazed clay beads by Elaine Ray, from Ornamentea, ornamentea.com)
- 42 in. (1.1m) silk cord
- 6 in. (15cm) 24-gauge half-hard wire
- **2** 12mm cones (Artbeads.com)
- lobster claw clasp and soldered jump ring
- chainnose and roundnose pliers
- diagonal wire cutters
- G-S Hypo Cement

One briolette has more than enough sparkle for this simple wire pendant with organic-looking wraps. Add minimalist earrings to keep things elegantly spare.

The one and only

Wire coils suspend a single bead for one-of-a-kind style

by Carol McKinney

Supply List

necklace
- 12mm briolette
- 16–18 in. (41–46cm) silk cord
- 15 in. (38cm) 24-gauge half-hard wire
- 5 in. (13cm) 20-gauge half-hard wire
- **3** 6mm split rings
- **2** crimp ends
- lobster claw clasp
- chainnose and roundnose pliers
- diagonal wire cutters
- split-ring pliers (optional)
- G-S Hypo Cement

earrings
- **2** 12mm briolettes
- 10 in. (25cm) 24-gauge half-hard wire
- chainnose and roundnose pliers
- diagonal wire cutters

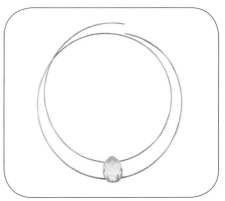

1 necklace • Cut a 15-in. (38cm) piece of 24-gauge wire. Center a briolette on the wire.

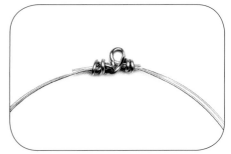

2 Overlap the ends of the 24-gauge wire. Wrap the ends tightly with 20-gauge wire, forming a loop with one of the wraps. Trim the excess 20-gauge wire.

3 Decide how long you want your necklace to be. (My necklaces are 17 in./43cm.) Cut a piece of silk cord to that length. On each end, apply glue and attach a crimp end (Basics).

4 Open a split ring (Basics) and attach the loop of the pendant. Center the split ring on the silk cord.

5 On one end, use a split ring to attach the crimp end and a lobster claw clasp. Attach a split ring to the other end.

EDITOR'S TIP

Save even more time by using pre-assembled necklace cord. Necklace cords are available in silk, rubber, suede, and leather.

1 earrings • Cut a 5-in. (13cm) piece of 24-gauge wire. String a briolette.

2 Using roundnose pliers, make a small loop on one end of the wire.

3 On the other end, bend ⅛ in. (3mm) of wire down at a right angle. Make a second earring to match the first.

Style at the touch of a button

Turquoise and gold unite in a quick bracelet and lariat

by Jane Konkel

A button clasp gives a simple turquoise-and-brushed-gold bracelet a little something extra. Add a chain lariat with a solitary drop on each end to complete the elegant set.

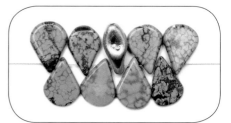

1 bracelet • Cut a piece of beading wire (Basics). (My bracelet is 7 in./18cm.) String four turquoise beads, a vermeil bead, and four turquoise beads. Center the beads on the wire.

2 On each end, string a vermeil bead and four turquoise beads. Repeat until the strand is within 2 in. (5cm) of the finished length. Check the fit, allowing 2 in. (5cm) for finishing. Add or remove beads from each end if necessary.

3 On one end, string: 3mm round spacer, 5mm rondelle, crimp bead, two round spacers, one hole of a button, rondelle, round spacer, rondelle, second hole of the button, round spacer. Go back through the round spacer, crimp bead, rondelle, and round spacer.

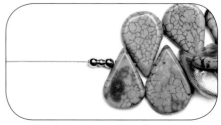

4 On the other end, string a round spacer, a crimp bead, and a round spacer.

5 To make a loop for the button, string a round spacer, four rondelles, a 4mm flat spacer, and four rondelles. String a flat spacer and four rondelles, repeating until the length equals the circumference of the button. End with a round spacer.

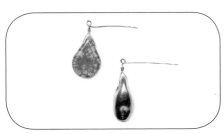

6 Go back through the round spacer, the crimp bead, and the round spacer. Tighten the wire, crimp the crimp beads (Basics), and trim the excess wire.

1 lariat • Cut a 3-in. (7.6cm) piece of wire. String a turquoise bead and make a set of wraps above it (Basics). Make the first half of a wrapped loop (Basics) above the wraps. Repeat with a vermeil bead.

2 Decide how long you want your lariat to be. (Mine is 44 in./1.1m.) Cut a piece of chain to that length. Attach a bead unit to each end of the chain and complete the wraps.

Supply List

bracelet
- **24–28** turquoise teardrop beads, top drilled, approximately 15 x 20mm
- **5–6** 20mm vermeil beads, top drilled (The Earth Bazaar, theearthbazaar.com)
- **23–31** 5mm turquoise rondelles
- **4–6** 4mm flat gold spacers
- **9** 3mm round gold spacers
- flexible beading wire, .014 or .015
- **2** crimp beads
- 28mm two-hole button, (Beads & Beyond, 425-462-8992)
- chainnose or crimping pliers
- diagonal wire cutters

lariat
- turquoise teardrop bead, top drilled, approximately 15 x 20mm
- 20mm vermeil bead, top drilled, (The Earth Bazaar, theearthbazaar.com)
- 6 in. (15cm) 24-gauge half-hard wire
- 40–48 in. (1–1.2m) chain, 2–4mm links
- chainnose and roundnose pliers
- diagonal wire cutters

Add personality with a floral focal piece

A nature-themed pendant inspires a chain-and-crystal necklace

by Lindsay Mikulsky

Pressed flowers backed by stained glass are a natural starting point for a quick necklace. Choose crystals in graduated hues, and attach the darkest ones near the pendant to highlight the focal point. Crystal-embellished ear threads carry on the color scheme.

Supply List

necklace
- 26mm stained-glass pendant (Fusion Beads, fusionbeads.com)
- **11** 6mm bicone crystals, **3** in color A, **4** in color B, **4** in color C
- 33 in. (84cm) 24-gauge half-hard wire
- 30–42 in. (76–106cm) chain, 3–4mm links
- **5** 4mm jump rings
- two-strand slide clasp
- chainnose and roundnose pliers
- diagonal wire cutters

earrings
- **6** 6mm bicone crystals, **2** in color A, **2** in color B, **2** in color C
- **2** 2-in. (5cm) decorative head pins
- pair of earring threads
- chainnose and roundnose pliers
- diagonal wire cutters

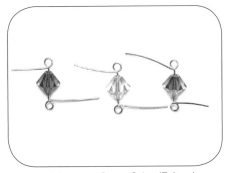

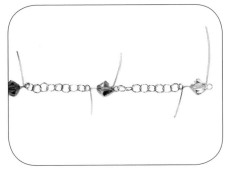

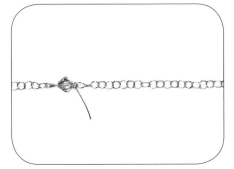

1 necklace • Cut a 3-in. (7.6cm) piece of wire. Make the first half of a wrapped loop (Basics) on one end. String a crystal. Make the first half of a wrapped loop. Repeat with the remaining crystals.

2 For the short strand: Cut four ¾-in. (1.9cm) pieces of chain. On each loop of a color A unit, attach a chain, a color B unit, a chain, and a color C unit. Complete the wraps, leaving the end loops unwrapped.

3 Decide how long you want your short strand to be. (Mine is 15 in./ 38cm.) Subtract the length of the segment from step 2, and cut a piece of chain to that length. Cut the chain in half. On each unwrapped loop, attach a chain and complete the wraps.

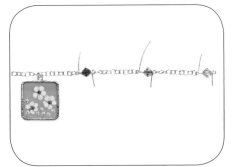

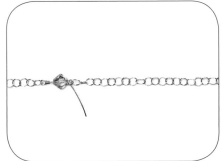

4 For the long strand: Cut a 2-in. (5cm) piece of chain. Open a jump ring (Basics) and attach a pendant and the center link. Close the jump ring.

5 Cut four 1-in. (2.5cm) pieces of chain. On each side of the pendant's chain, attach: color A unit, chain, color B unit, chain, color C unit. Complete the wraps, leaving the end loops unwrapped.

6 Decide how long you want your long strand to be. (Mine is 18 in./ 46cm.) Subtract the length of the segment from step 5, and cut a piece of chain to that length. Cut the chain in half. On each unwrapped loop, attach a chain and complete the wraps.

7 Check the fit, and trim chain from each end if necessary. On each end, use a jump ring to attach the chain to the corresponding loop of half of the clasp.

1 earrings • On a decorative head pin, string a color A crystal, a color B crystal, and a color C crystal. Make the first half of a wrapped loop (Basics).

2 Attach the dangle to the loop of an earring thread. Complete the wraps. Make a second earring to match the first.

Briolette bangle

Attach briolettes to a bracelet form for a stylish bangle

by Debbi Simon

Gemstone briolettes and metal accent beads come together easily with a premade bangle. This design is more fun than formal, so enjoy the process of creating an asymmetrical bead arrangement.

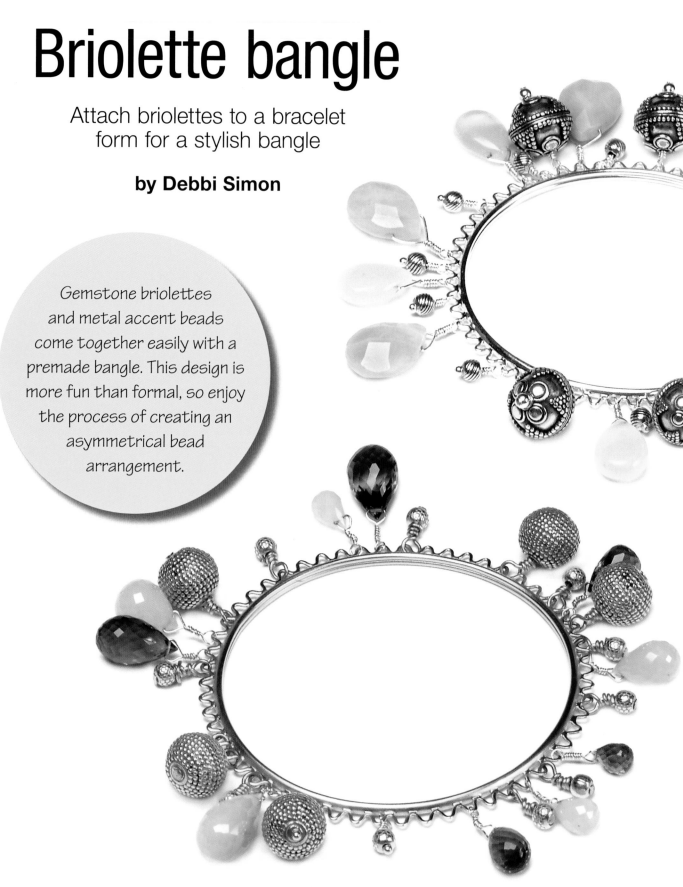

1 On your work space, arrange beads around a bangle. The bracelet's weight should be somewhat balanced, but a symmetrical pattern isn't necessary.

2 On a head pin, string an accent bead and make the first half of a wrapped loop (Basics). If the accent bead's hole is large, string a spacer before stringing the accent bead or use a decorative head pin. Repeat with the remaining accent beads.

3 Cut a 3-in. (7.6cm) piece of wire. String a top-drilled bead and make a set of wraps above it (Basics). Make the first half of a wrapped loop above the wraps. If the bead is flat, make the loop perpendicular to the bead. Repeat with the remaining top-drilled beads.

4 Attach the bead units to the bangle's loops. There will be more loops than bead units, so cluster the bead units in one- to five-loop groups, leaving the loops empty in between. Complete the wraps as you attach each bead unit.

EDITOR'S TIP

Whiskey topaz and chrysoprase complement a gold bangle's warm tones. A silver bangle stays cool with amazonite and hemimorphite.

WHERE TO SHOP

Bangles are available from Nina Designs, ninadesigns.com, in silver, gold plate, and vermeil.

Supply List

- **8–12** 8–20mm top-drilled beads
- **5–6** 10–14mm accent beads
- **10–12** 4–5mm accent beads
- 3mm round spacers for each large-hole bead (optional)
- 3-in. (7.6cm) bangle bracelet with ruffled-loop edge
- 24–36 in. (61–90cm) 24- or 26-gauge half-hard wire
- **15–18** 2-in. (5cm) head pins
- 2-in. (5cm) decorative head pins for each large-hole bead (optional)
- chainnose and roundnose pliers
- diagonal wire cutters

Wear your hearts on your sleeve

Mix vintage hearts in a bracelet and earrings

by Naomi Fujimoto

Check out any thrift store, and you'll find lots of pre-loved jewelry with hearts — especially necklaces and earrings. Buy an assortment: silver and gold, flat and puffy, big and small. Combine them all in a timeless bracelet, then add chunky Lucite earrings.

1 bracelet • Cut a piece of bracelet-length chain. On your work space, arrange the charms and earrings along the chain. Balance different colors, shapes, sizes, and textures. Leave links between charms available for beads.

2 To make a charm from a post earring: Using roundnose pliers, make a loop with the earring post. Try not to overwork the wire, as it may become brittle. The earring can now be attached with a jump ring.

3 Open a jump ring (Basics). Attach a charm to the center chain link. Close the jump ring. Use jump rings to attach the remaining charms as desired.

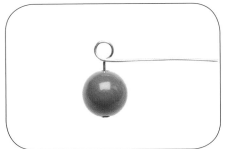

4 On a head pin, string a bead. Make the first half of a wrapped loop (Basics). Repeat to make the desired number of bead units.

5 For each top-drilled bead, cut a 3-in. (7.6cm) piece of wire. String the bead and make a set of wraps above it (Basics). Make the first half of a wrapped loop.

DESIGN OPTION

If you want to skip the thrift-store shopping, try Pocket Hearts from Thomas Mann, thomasmann.com.

6 Attach each bead unit to the chain as desired. Complete the wraps.

7 Check the fit, and trim chain from each end if necessary. Use a jump ring to attach half of the clasp to each end. If desired, attach a charm or a bead to the loop half of the clasp.

1 earrings • On a head pin, string a bead. Make the first half of a wrapped loop (Basics).

2 Cut a 1–2-in. (2.5–5cm) piece of chain. Attach the bead unit and complete the wraps.

3 Open a jump ring (Basics). Attach the dangle and the loop of an earring wire. Close the jump ring. Make a second earring to match the first.

Supply List

bracelet
- **7–15** 15–35mm heart-shaped charms or earrings
- **8–20** 8–16mm beads
- 3 in. (7.6cm) 22-gauge half-hard wire (for each top-drilled bead)
- 6½–8 in. (16.5–20cm) chain, 7–10mm links (Ornamentea, ornamentea.com)
- **8–20** 2-in. (5cm) 22-gauge head pins
- **9–17** 5–6mm 18- or 20-gauge jump rings
- 3–4mm jump rings (optional, see Editor's Tips)

- toggle clasp
- chainnose and roundnose pliers
- diagonal wire cutters
- additional pair of chainnose pliers (optional)

earrings
- **2** 8–16mm beads
- 2–3 in. (5–7.6cm) chain, 7–10mm links (Ornamentea, ornamentea.com)
- **2** 2-in. (5cm) 22-gauge head pins
- **2** 4–6mm jump rings
- pair of earring wires
- chainnose and roundnose pliers
- diagonal wire cutters

EDITOR'S TIPS

- You can use oval jump rings instead of round ones.
- To give a charm more room to hang from the chain, attach one or more 3–4mm jump rings between the charm and the larger jump ring.

Do
the twist

Big beads make for a snappy necklace, bracelet, and earrings

by Naomi Fujimoto

For a knockout necklace, mix gemstones with smooth and faceted textures. Pick out the strand of big beads first, then combine it with strands in other shapes, sizes, and colors. Try brights and neutrals together, or make a monochromatic version.

FAST

EDITOR'S TIP

The necklace's strands must taper so that the bar half of the clasp fits through the loop half. If necessary, string additional 3–4mm spacers on each end before stringing the crimp bead.

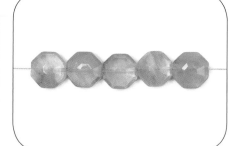

1 **necklace** • Cut five pieces of beading wire (Basics). (My necklace is 18 in./46cm.) On one wire, string beads until the strand is within 3 in. (7.6cm) of the finished length.

2 On each remaining wire, string beads until the strand is within 3 in. (7.6cm) of the finished length. The strands should be approximately equal in length; use the strand with the largest beads to gauge the length of the others.

3 On one side, on each end, string: two 5–6mm spacers, 3–4mm spacer, crimp bead, 3–4mm spacer, half of the clasp. Go back through the last few beads strung and tighten the wire.

4 Repeat step 3 on the other side, leaving approximately ¼ in. (6mm) of extra wire between the first spacer and the crimp bead. (You'll need the extra length so you can twist the finished strands.) Check the fit, and add or remove beads if necessary. Crimp the crimp beads (Basics) and trim the excess wire.

1 **bracelet** • Cut two pieces of beading wire (Basics). On each wire, string beads until the strand is within 1½ in. (3.8cm) of the finished length.

2 On each end, string: 5–6mm spacer, one or two 3–4mm spacers, crimp bead, 3–4mm spacer, half of the clasp. Check the fit, and add or remove beads if necessary. Go back through the last few beads strung and tighten the wire. Crimp the crimp bead (Basics) and trim the excess wire.

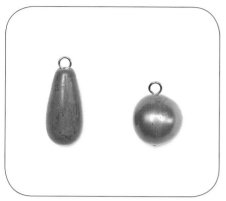

1 earrings • On a head pin, string a bead. Make a plain loop (Basics). Repeat with a second bead in a different style.

2 Cut a ½–1-in. (1.3–2.5cm) piece of chain. Open the loop of an earring wire (Basics) and attach the chain. Close the loop.

3 Open the loop of the larger bead unit (Basics) and attach the end link of chain. Close the loop. Attach the remaining bead unit to the chain. Make a second earring in the mirror image of the first.

Supply List

necklace
- **5** 16-in. (41cm) strands 10–25mm beads, in different colors and shapes
- **20** 5–6mm spacers
- **20–40** 3–4mm spacers
- flexible beading wire, .018 or .019
- **10** crimp beads
- large toggle clasp
- chainnose or crimping pliers
- diagonal wire cutters

bracelet
- **2** 16-in. (41cm) strands 10–25mm beads, in two styles
- **4** 5–6mm spacers
- **4–8** 3–4mm spacers
- flexible beading wire, .018 or .019
- **4** crimp beads
- toggle clasp
- chainnose or crimping pliers
- diagonal wire cutters

earrings
- **4** 10–25mm beads, in two styles, left over from bracelet
- 1–2 in. (2.5–5cm) chain, 3–4mm links
- **4** 1½-in. (3.8cm) head pins
- pair of earring wires
- chainnose and roundnose pliers
- diagonal wire cutters

DESIGN OPTIONS

- String four strands instead of five if the necklace feels too heavy. Use the fifth strand to make a two-strand bracelet.
- Try a monochromatic necklace. I used amazonite, chalcedony, turquoise, and simulated aquamarine in mine.
- Make simple drop earrings with single leftover gemstones.

With a few swift hammer blows, some sharp turns with pliers, and a few beads, you can quickly create a jaunty set of dangles. Grouped together on an earring wire, this spirited trio provides instant color and style.

Zigzag dangles

Showcase bright beads on striking earrings

by Wendy Witchner

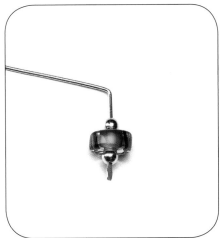

1 Cut three 3-in. (7.6cm) pieces of wire. With one or two strikes, hammer the tip of each wire into a paddle shape. File the edges.

2 On one wire, string a 3mm round, a furnace-glass disc, and a 3mm. On the other wires, string a 2mm round, a 4mm bicone, and a 2mm.

3 Begin with the furnace-glass dangle. With chainnose pliers, bend the wire about 2mm above the top bead.

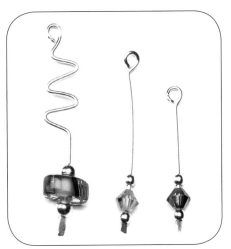

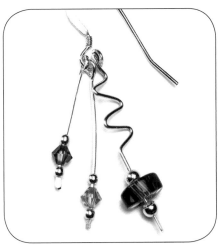

4 Bend the wire back to begin a zigzag pattern. Continue until the zigzag portion is about ¾-in. (2cm) long.

5 Trim the zigzag wire ⅜ in. (1cm) above the top bend and make a plain loop (Basics). Trim one of the other wires to 1⅜ in. (3.5cm) and the third wire to 1⅛ in. (2.9cm). Make a plain loop at the end of each wire.

6 Open the loop on an earring wire and attach the dangles, stringing the shortest first and the zigzag last. Close the loop. Make a second earring to match the first.

Supply List

- 18 in. (46cm) 20-gauge wire
- **2** 6–8mm furnace-glass discs
- **4** 4mm bicone crystals, **2** each of 2 colors
- **4** 3mm round beads
- **8** 2mm round beads
- pair of earring wires
- chainnose and roundnose pliers
- diagonal wire cutters
- ball peen hammer
- bench block
- metal file

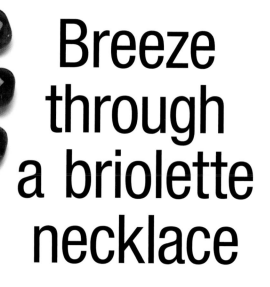

Breeze through a briolette necklace

A simple pattern makes short work of stringing a two-strand necklace

by Lindsay Mikulsky

Labradorite briolettes are the perfect focus for a sophisticated necklace that's make-and-wear friendly. Tiny labradorite and garnet rounds separate the briolettes, but you can still string this basic pattern quickly.

1 necklace • Cut a piece of beading wire (Basics) for the short strand of your necklace. Cut a second piece 2 in. (5cm) longer than the first.

On the short wire, string a 4mm round bead and a 2mm round bead. Repeat until the strand is within 1 in. (2.5cm) of the finished length.

2 a On the long wire, center a briolette.

b On each end, string a 2mm, a 4mm, a 2mm, and a briolette. Repeat until the strand is within 1 in. (2.5cm) of the finished length. End with a 4mm.

3 On each end of each strand, string a spacer, a crimp bead, a spacer, and the corresponding loop of half of the clasp. Check the fit, and add or remove beads if necessary. Go back through the beads just strung and tighten the wire. Crimp the crimp bead (Basics) and trim the excess wire.

1 earrings • Cut a 3-in. (7.6cm) piece of wire. String a briolette and make a set of wraps above it (Basics). Make the first half of a wrapped loop (Basics) above the wraps.

3 Cut two ½-in. (1.3cm) pieces of chain. Attach one piece to the briolette unit and a loop of the round-bead unit. Attach the other piece to the remaining loop of the round-bead unit. Complete the wraps.

2 Cut a 2½-in. (6.4cm) piece of wire. Make the first half of a wrapped loop. String a 2mm round bead, a 4mm round bead, and a 2mm. Make the first half of a wrapped loop.

4 Open the loop of an earring wire (Basics). Attach the dangle and close the loop. Make a second earring to match the first.

Supply List

necklace (strands are 15 in./38cm and 17 in./43 cm)
- 16-in. (41cm) strand 10mm gemstone briolettes
- 16-in. (41cm) strand 4mm faceted round gemstone beads
- 16-in. (41cm) strand 2mm round gemstone beads
- 8 3mm round spacers
- flexible beading wire, .014 or .015
- 4 crimp beads
- two-strand clasp
- chainnose or crimping pliers
- diagonal wire cutters

earrings
- 2 10mm gemstone briolettes
- 2 4mm faceted round gemstone beads
- 4 2mm round gemstone beads
- 11 in. (28cm) 24-gauge half-hard wire
- 2 in. (5cm) chain, 3–4mm links
- pair of earring wires
- chainnose and roundnose pliers
- diagonal wire cutters

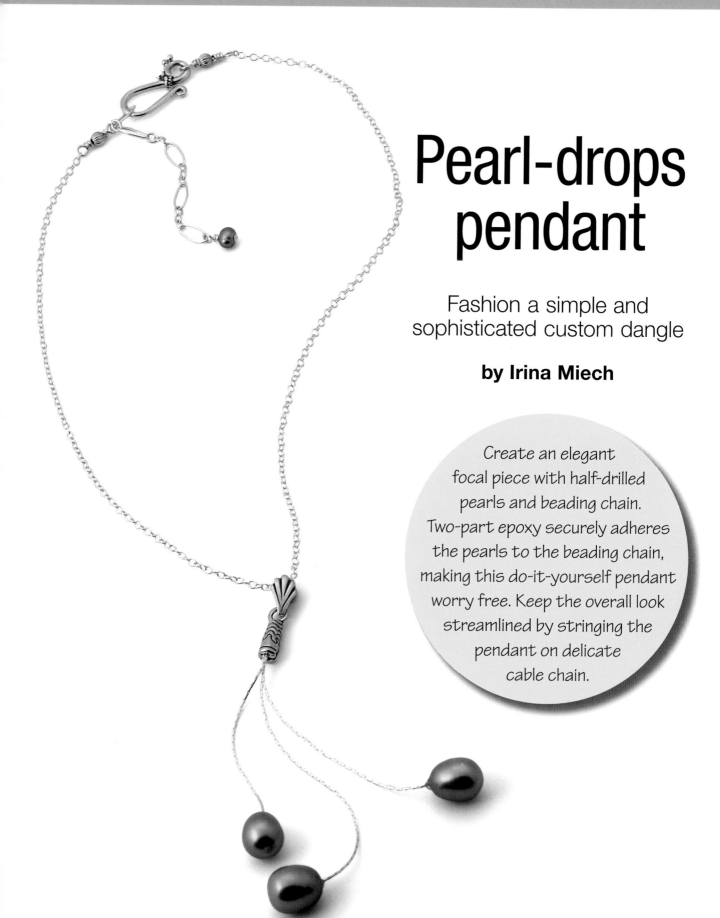

Pearl-drops pendant

Fashion a simple and sophisticated custom dangle

by Irina Miech

Create an elegant focal piece with half-drilled pearls and beading chain. Two-part epoxy securely adheres the pearls to the beading chain, making this do-it-yourself pendant worry free. Keep the overall look streamlined by stringing the pendant on delicate cable chain.

1 necklace • Cut a 2-in. (5cm), 2¼-in. (5.7cm), and 2¾-in. (7cm) piece of beading chain.

Prepare two-part epoxy and put a small amount in three half-drilled pearls. Insert a piece of beading chain into each pearl and let dry.

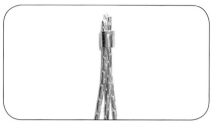

2 String a crimp tube over all three pieces of beading chain. Position the crimp tube near the ends of the chains and make a folded crimp (Basics).

3 String a crimp cone over the folded crimp. Use chainnose pliers to close the crimp cone.

4 Attach the crimp cone's loop to a bail. Use chainnose pliers to close the bail's loop.

5 Decide how long you want your necklace to be (excluding the length of the pendant) and cut a piece of cable chain to that length. Center the pendant on the chain.

6 Cut a 3-in. (7.6cm) piece of wire. Make the first half of a wrapped loop (Basics) on one end. String a spacer, and make the first half of a wrapped loop. Make two spacer units.

7 On one end of the chain, use a spacer unit to attach a hook clasp. Complete the wraps.

Repeat on the other end, substituting a 2-in. (5cm) piece of large-link chain for the clasp.

8 On a head pin, string a 4–5mm pearl and make the first half of a wrapped loop. Attach the pearl unit to the extender chain and complete the wraps.

Supply List

All supplies from Eclectica, (262) 641-0910.

necklace
- **3** 9–12mm half-drilled pearls
- 4–5mm pearl
- **2** 2–3mm round spacers
- 6 in. (15cm) 24-gauge half-hard wire
- 12–18 in. (30–46cm) cable chain, 1.5–2 mm links
- 7 in. (18cm) beading chain
- 1½-in. (3.8cm) head pin
- 2mm crimp tube
- 12mm crimp cone
- 8–10mm bail
- hook clasp

- 2-in. (5cm) chain for extender, 5–7mm links
- chainnose and roundnose pliers
- crimping pliers
- diagonal wire cutters
- two-part clear-drying epoxy

earrings
- **6** 4–5mm pearls
- 1 in. (2.5cm) cable chain, 1.5–2mm links
- **6** 1-in. (2.5cm) head pins
- **2** 3–4mm jump rings
- pair of earring threads
- chainnose and roundnose pliers
- diagonal wire cutters

EDITOR'S TIP

For necklace step 1, use a toothpick to put a tiny drop of epoxy in each pearl.

1 **earrings** • On a head pin, string a 4–5mm pearl. Make a plain loop (Basics). Make three pearl units.

2 Cut a six-link piece of chain. Open the loop of a pearl unit (Basics) and attach it to one end. Close the loop. Attach the two remaining pearl units to every other link of chain.

3 Open a jump ring (Basics). Attach the dangle and the loop of an earring thread. Close the jump ring. Make a second earring to match the first.

FASTER

· under 30 minutes ·

If you don't think "fast" is fast enough, we've designed some speedier options, like a necklace and earrings made with Venetian glass (page 56), textured wooden beads (page 58), or center-drilled coin pearls (page 46). For multiple style options, try the briolette necklace with detachable strands (page 40).

Easy as 1-2-3

String a simple multistrand look with finished chains

by Cathy Jakicic

You can quickly string three necklaces in graduated lengths using chains with clasps already attached. Wear the necklaces together or individually for different looks. Leftover chain adds swing to matching earrings.

1 necklaces • For the shortest necklace, cut a 7-in. (18cm) piece of beading wire. Center a briolette on the wire.

2 On each end, string a rondelle and a briolette. Repeat twice and then string a rondelle, for a total of seven briolettes and eight rondelles.

1 earrings • Cut a 3-in. (7.6cm) piece of wire. String a briolette and make a set of wraps above it (Basics). Make the first half of a wrapped loop above the wraps (Basics).

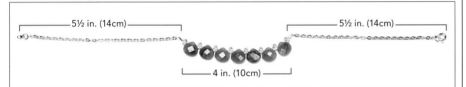

5½ in. (14cm) — 5½ in. (14cm) —

— 4 in. (10cm) —

3 a Decide how long you want your necklace to be. (Mine is 15 in./38cm.) Subtract the length of the beaded portion. Divide the remaining number in half, and cut that length from each end of a finished chain. (See diagram above.)

b On each end of the wire, string a crimp bead and a chain. Check the fit and trim chain if necessary. Go back through the last few beads strung and tighten the wire. Crimp the crimp bead (Basics) and trim the excess wire.

2 Cut a 1½-in. (3.8cm) piece of chain. Attach the bead unit and complete the wraps. Open the loop of an earring wire (Basics). Attach the dangle and close the loop. Make a second earring to match the first.

4 For the mid-length necklace: Cut an 8-in. (20cm) piece of beading wire. Center an alternating pattern of ten rondelles and nine briolettes on the wire. Cut two chain segments, each ½ in. (1.3cm) longer than those of the shortest necklace.

For the longest necklace, increase the length of the beaded portion and chain in the same increments.

Repeat step 3b to complete the strands.

Supply List

necklaces
- 16-in. (41cm) strand 13mm faceted briolettes, top drilled
- **30** 6mm crystal rondelles
- flexible beading wire, .014 or .015
- **3** 24-in. (61cm) finished chains
- **6** crimp beads
- chainnose or crimping pliers
- diagonal wire cutters

earrings
- **2** 13mm faceted briolettes, top drilled
- 6 in. (15cm) 24-gauge half-hard wire
- 3 in. (7.6cm) chain, left over from necklaces
- pair of earring wires
- chainnose and roundnose pliers
- diagonal wire cutters

Subtle style

An understated necklace design is easily adapted to a bracelet

by Beth Stone

When you want to issue your fashion statement quickly and quietly, this delicate necklace-and-bracelet set fits the bill. Want to turn up the volume a bit? Just choose brighter or contrasting colors.

1 necklace • Cut a piece of beading wire (Basics). (My necklaces are 16 in./41cm.) On the wire, center: flat spacer, rondelle, flat spacer, top-drilled pearl, flat spacer, rondelle, flat spacer.

2 On each end, string: five 13º seed beads, flat spacer, rondelle, flat spacer, top-drilled pearl, flat spacer, rondelle, flat spacer. Repeat twice on each end.

3 On each end, string 10 13ºs, a flat spacer, a round pearl, and a flat spacer.

Repeat twice, stringing five additional 13ºs in each sequence.

4 On each end, string 13ºs until the strand is within 1 in. (2.5cm) of the finished length.

On one end, string two round spacers, a crimp bead, and a lobster claw clasp. Repeat on the other end, substituting a soldered jump ring for the clasp. Check the fit, and add or remove beads from each end if necessary. Go back through the beads just strung. Tighten the wire and crimp the crimp beads (Basics). Trim the excess wire.

EDITOR'S TIP

Use a magnetic clasp for the bracelet to make it easier to put on and take off.

Supply List

necklace
- **14–18** 6mm rondelles
- **7–9** 6mm pearls, top drilled
- **6–8** 4mm round pearls
- **1g** 13º seed beads
- **40–52** 4mm flat spacers
- **4** 3mm round spacers
- flexible beading wire, .014 or .015
- **2** crimp beads
- lobster claw clasp and soldered jump ring
- chainnose or crimping pliers
- diagonal wire cutters

bracelet
- **12–20** 6mm rondelles
- **5–9** 6mm pearls, top drilled
- **1g** 13º seed beads
- **24–40** 4mm flat spacers
- flexible beading wire, .014 or .015
- **2** crimp beads
- clasp
- chainnose or crimping pliers
- diagonal wire cutters

1 bracelet • Cut a piece of beading wire (Basics). String: flat spacer, rondelle, flat spacer, top-drilled pearl, flat spacer, rondelle, flat spacer, five 13º seed beads. Repeat until the strand is within 1 in. (2.5cm) of the finished length. End with a flat spacer, a rondelle, and a flat spacer.

2 On each end, string a crimp bead and half of the clasp. Check the fit, and add or remove beads from each end if necessary. Go back through the last few beads strung. Tighten the wire and crimp the crimp bead (Basics). Trim the excess wire.

This sharp curve won't slow you down

Textured beads add depth to a simple curved design

by Cathy Jakicic

Take the time to find unusual materials, and you'll be able to put together a distinctive design in a snap. A sturdy chain will balance the dominant curve of the beads and allow you to avoid attaching jump rings when finishing.

1 Cut one coil of memory wire. Center three spacers, two felt beads, and three spacers.

2 On each end, string three felt beads, three spacers, two felt beads, and six spacers. Make a loop.

3 Decide how long you want your necklace to be. (Mine is 17 in./ 43cm.) Subtract 3 in. (7.6cm) and cut a piece of chain to that length. Cut the chain in half. On each end of the memory wire, open the loop and attach a chain. Close the loop.

4 On each end, carefully cut one side of the link. Open the link as if it were a jump ring (Basics). Attach half of the clasp and close the link.

EDITOR'S TIP

Remember to cut memory wire with heavy-duty wire cutters. Alternately, use chainnose pliers to bend the wire back and forth until it breaks.

Supply List

- **12** 12mm felt beads
- **24** 6mm flat spacers
- memory wire, bracelet diameter (2 in./5cm)
- 13–15 in. (33–38) heavy cable chain, 10–12mm links
- toggle clasp
- chainnose and roundnose pliers
- heavy-duty wire cutters

DESIGN OPTIONS

Using beads with different textures gives the necklace a completely new look. Metallic and lava beads are available from Eclectica, (262) 641-0910.

String a shimmery strand

Coin pearls add gleaming elegance to an easy necklace and earrings

by Rupa Balachandar

For quick sophistication, center a marcasite-and-amber tube bead among unusual center-drilled coin pearls. Silver spacers highlight the shape and iridescence of the individual pearls. Matching earrings complete your speedy set.

EDITOR'S TIP

Infuse the earrings with color by using rondelles that match the focal bead.

1 **necklace •** Cut a piece of beading wire (Basics). (My necklace is 17 in./43cm.) Center a small (3–5mm) spacer, a focal bead, and a small spacer.

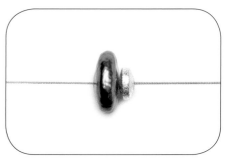

2 On each end, string a pearl and a large (6–8mm) spacer. Repeat six to eight times.

1 **earrings** • On a decorative head pin, string a rondelle, a pearl, and a spacer. Make a wrapped loop (Basics).

2 Open the loop of an earring wire (Basics). Attach the dangle and close the loop. Make a second earring to match the first.

Supply List

necklace
• 30–35mm focal bead
• 16-in. (41cm) strand 12–15mm coin pearls, center drilled
• **14-18** 6–8mm flat spacers
• **40-50** 3–5mm flat spacers
• **4** 3mm round spacers
• flexible beading wire, .014 or .015
• **2** crimp beads
• French (bullion) wire
• toggle clasp
• chainnose or crimping pliers
• diagonal wire cutters

earrings
• **2** 12–15mm coin pearls, center drilled
• **2** 4mm rondelles
• **2** 6–8mm flat spacers
• **2** 2-in. (5cm) decorative head pins
• pair of decorative earring wires
• chainnose and roundnose pliers
• diagonal wire cutters

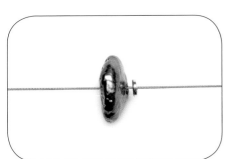

3 On each end, string a pearl and a small spacer. Repeat until the strand is within 1 in. (2.5cm) of the finished length. Check the fit, and add or remove beads from each end if necessary.

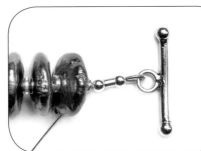

4 Cut two ⅜-in. (1cm) pieces of French (bullion) wire. On each end, string: round spacer, crimp bead, round spacer, French wire, half of the clasp. Go back through the beads just strung and tighten the wire. Crimp the crimp beads (Basics) and trim the excess wire.

Think inside the box

Cut-out gemstones make a fashionable framework for a bracelet and earrings

by Andrea Loss

Diamond-shaped gemstones border smaller beads in a wide bracelet that's saturated with mossy green color. Coordinate a pair of earrings, and see this ensemble take shape.

1 **bracelet** • Cut a piece of beading wire (Basics). String: one hole of an open-center bead, round spacer, lentil bead, round spacer, second hole of the open-center bead. Center the beads on the wire.

2 On each end, string: flat spacer, one hole of an open-center bead, round spacer, lentil, round spacer, second hole of the open-center bead. Repeat. String flat spacers until the bracelet is within 1 in. (2.5cm) of the finished length.

3 On each end, string a crimp bead, a flat spacer, and half of the clasp. Check the fit, and add or remove beads from each end if necessary. Go back through the last few beads strung and tighten the wire. Crimp the crimp bead (Basics) and trim the excess wire.

1 **open-center earrings** • On a head pin, string a round spacer, one hole of an open-center bead, and a flat spacer. Make a wrapped loop (Basics).

2 Open the loop of an earring wire (Basics) and attach the dangle. Close the loop. Make a second earring to match the first.

Supply List

bracelet
- **5** 26mm open-center beads (Midwest Beads, midwestbeads.biz)
- **5** 10mm lentil beads
- **8–20** 4mm flat spacers
- **10** 3mm round spacers
- flexible beading wire, .014 or .015
- **2** crimp beads
- toggle clasp
- chainnose or crimping pliers
- diagonal wire cutters

open-center earrings
- **2** 26mm open-center beads (Midwest Beads, midwestbeads.biz)
- **2** 4mm flat spacers
- **2** 3mm round spacers
- **2** 1½-in. (3.8cm) head pins
- pair of earring wires
- chainnose and roundnose pliers
- diagonal wire cutters

lentil earrings
- **2** 10mm lentil beads
- **4** 4mm flat spacers
- **4** 3mm round spacers
- **2** 1½-in. (3.8cm) head pins
- pair of earring wires
- chainnose and roundnose pliers
- diagonal wire cutters

1 **lentil earrings** • On a head pin, string: round spacer, flat spacer, lentil bead, flat spacer, round spacer. Make a plain loop (Basics).

2 Open the loop of an earring wire (Basics) and attach the dangle. Close the loop. Make a second earring to match the first.

DESIGN OPTION

If you like, include additional beads in the open-center earrings — just consider how much they'll weigh.

Add sparkle in a flash

A mix of crystals adorns a delicate chain necklace

by Catherine Hodge

A few crystal dangles add flash to a two-strand chain necklace. Use large cosmic crystals as pendants and round and bicone crystals to add brilliant flashes. It only takes a few minutes to make dangle earrings that mimic the necklace's design.

1 necklace • To make a crystal unit: On a head pin, string a cosmic crystal. Make the first half of a wrapped loop (Basics). Repeat with the second cosmic crystal and both the bicone and round crystals.

3 Decide how long you want your two necklace strands to be. (My sliver necklace has 14 in./ 36cm and 20 in./51cm strands; my gold necklace has 17 in./43cm and 20 in./51cm. strands) Cut a piece of chain to each length.

On each piece of chain, attach a cosmic unit to the center link. Attach a ¾-in. (1.9cm) piece of chain, a round unit, and a bicone unit to the cosmic unit's loop. Complete the wraps.

2 Cut two 1½-in. (3.8cm), two 1¼-in. (3.2cm), and two ¾-in. (1.9cm) pieces of chain. Attach each 1½-in. (3.8cm) piece to a bicone unit and each 1¼-in. (3.2cm) piece to a round unit. Complete the wraps.

4 Check the fit, and trim chain from each end if necessary. On each end, attach a split ring (Basics) to both chains. On one side, attach a lobster claw clasp to the split ring.

Supply List

necklace
- **2** 16mm cosmic crystals
- **2** 6mm bicone crystals
- **2** 4mm round crystals
- 38–48 in. (.97–1.2m) long-and-short-link chain, 3–4mm links
- **6** 2-in. (5cm) head pins
- **2** 4–6mm split rings
- lobster claw clasp
- chainnose and roundnose pliers
- diagonal wire cutters
- split-ring pliers (optional)

earrings
- **2** 6mm bicone crystals
- **2** 4mm round crystals
- 8 in. (20cm) long-and-short-link chain, 3–4mm links
- **2** 2-in. (5cm) head pins
- pair of earring wires
- chainnose and roundnose pliers
- diagonal wire cutters

WHERE TO SHOP

Find crystals for these projects at JewelrySupply.com.

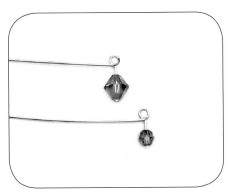

1 earrings • On a head pin, string a bicone crystal. Make the first half of a wrapped loop (Basics). Repeat with a round crystal.

2 Repeat step 2 of the necklace, but make only one of each chain unit.

3 Open the loop of an earring wire (Basics). Attach each chain unit. Close the loop. Make a second earring to match the first.

Boulder dash

Sprint through a necklace by focusing on big beads

by Cari Rosen

Maximize
your efforts by pairing
large gemstones with smaller
beads for a shapely necklace.
Unify your design by choosing
drops and tube beads to match
a secondary color in the
gemstones.

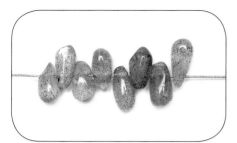

1 Cut a piece of beading wire (Basics). (My necklaces are 16 in./41cm.) Center eight top-drilled beads on the wire.

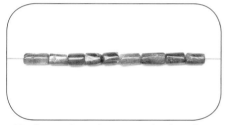

2 On each end, string a focal bead, eight top-drilled beads, and a focal bead.

3 On each end, string tube beads until the necklace is within 1 in. (2.5cm) of the finished length.

4 On one end, string a crimp bead, a spacer, and a lobster claw clasp. Repeat on the other end, substituting a soldered jump ring for the clasp. Check the fit, and add or remove beads from each end if necessary. On each end, go back through the last few beads strung and tighten the wire. Crimp the crimp bead (Basics) and trim the excess wire. Using chainnose pliers, close a crimp cover over the crimp bead.

DESIGN OPTION

For a different look, make the piece with faceted rondelles instead of tube beads.

Supply List

- **4** 30mm focal beads
- 16-in. (41cm) strand 8–12mm beads, top drilled
- 16-in. (41cm) strand 8–12mm tube beads
- **2** 6mm spacers
- flexible beading wire, .014 or .015
- **2** crimp beads
- **2** crimp covers
- lobster claw clasp and soldered jump ring
- chainnose pliers
- diagonal wire cutters
- crimping pliers (optional)

Steer by the stars

Connect charms and beads to make a celestial bracelet and earrings

by Jane Konkel

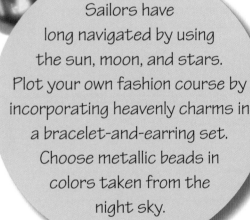

Sailors have long navigated by using the sun, moon, and stars. Plot your own fashion course by incorporating heavenly charms in a bracelet-and-earring set. Choose metallic beads in colors taken from the night sky.

1 **bracelet** • On a head pin, string a 12mm bead and make the first half of a wrapped loop (Basics). Repeat with the remaining beads.

2 Decide how long you want your bracelet to be, and cut a piece of chain to that length. Open a jump ring (Basics). Attach the largest charm and the chain's center link. Close the jump ring.

3 On each side, skip a link and attach the loop of a bead unit. Complete the wraps.

4 Attach charms and bead units to every other link. Check the fit, allowing 1 in. (2.5cm) for finishing. Trim chain from each end if necessary.

5 On one end, use a jump ring to attach the loop half of a toggle clasp.

6 On the other end, use two jump rings to attach the bar half of the clasp.

Supply List

bracelet
- **5–7** 12–30mm charms
- **5–7** 12mm metallic beads
- 6½–8 in. (16.5–20cm) brass chain, 6–10mm links
- **5–7** 2-in. (5cm) head pins
- **8–10** 6mm jump rings
- toggle clasp
- chainnose and roundnose pliers
- diagonal wire cutters

earrings
- **2** 12–15mm charms
- **2** 12mm metallic beads
- 1 in. (2.5cm) brass chain, 6–10mm links
- **2** 1½-in. (3.8cm) eye pins
- pair of earring wires
- chainnose and roundnose pliers
- diagonal wire cutters

WHERE TO SHOP

The nickel-free brass chain, charms, and findings are available wholesale at Vintaj Natural Brass Co., vintaj.com. Check the Web site for retail sales options.

1 **earrings** • Open the loop of an eye pin (Basics) and attach a charm. Close the loop.

2 String a bead and make the first half of a wrapped loop (Basics).

3 Cut a link of chain. Attach the link and the loop. Complete the wraps.

4 Open the loop of an earring wire (Basics). Attach the dangle and close the loop. Make a second earring with a different charm.

Maximum impact, minimal effort

Group Venetian-glass focal beads at the front of a chain necklace

by Lindsay Mikulsky

Using chain to finish a short beaded strand saves time, reduces cost, and strikes a fashionable balance between vibrant color and classic metals. Whip up a pair of matching earrings in just a few extra minutes.

1 necklace • Cut a 12-in. (30cm) piece of beading wire. On the wire, center: 7mm saucer bead, 12mm disc bead, 9mm saucer bead, 20mm discbead, 9mm saucer, 12mm disc, 7mm saucer.

2 On each end, string: 8mm color A round bead, 6mm saucer bead, 8mm color B round bead, 6mm saucer, 8mm color A round, 6mm saucer, 6mm color B round bead.

Supply List

necklace
- 20mm Venetian-glass disc bead
- **2** 12mm Venetian-glass disc beads
- **6** 8mm Venetian-glass round beads, **4** in color A, **2** in color B
- **2** 6mm Venetian-glass round beads, in color B
- **2** 9mm saucer beads
- **2** 7mm saucer beads
- **6** 6mm saucer beads
- **4** 3mm round spacers
- flexible beading wire, .014 or .015
- 16–24 in. (41–61cm) chain, in two styles, 3–7mm links
- **4** 4–5mm oval jump rings
- **2** crimp beads
- **2** crimp covers
- box clasp
- chainnose and roundnose pliers, or **2** pairs of chainnose pliers
- diagonal wire cutters
- crimping pliers (optional)

earrings
- **2** 8mm Venetian-glass round beads
- **2** 6mm round spacers
- **4** 3mm round spacers
- 6 in. (15cm) 22- or 24-gauge half-hard wire
- **2** 1½-in. (3.8cm) head pins
- **4** 4–5mm oval jump rings
- pair of earring wires
- chainnose and roundnose pliers
- diagonal wire cutters

3 On each end, string a 3mm spacer, a crimp bead, a 3mm spacer, and a jump ring. Go back through the beads just strung and tighten the wire. Crimp the crimp bead (Basics) and trim the excess wire. Close a crimp cover over the crimp.

4 Decide how long you want your necklace to be. (Mine is 16 in./ 41cm.) Subtract the length of the beaded strand, and cut two pieces of chain, in different styles, to that length. Cut each piece in half.

On each end of the beaded strand, open the jump ring (Basics) and attach two different chains. Close the jump ring.

5 Check the fit, and trim chain from each end if necessary. On each end, use a jump ring to attach both pieces of chain to half of the clasp.

WHERE TO SHOP

- Venetian-glass beads are available from Gems2Behold, gems2behold.com.
- Gold-filled beads, chain, and findings are available from Artbeads.com.

1 earrings • On a head pin, string an 8mm round bead. Make a wrapped loop (Basics).

2 Cut a 3-in. (7.6cm) piece of wire. Make a wrapped loop on one end. String a 3mm spacer, a 6mm spacer, and a 3mm spacer. Make a wrapped loop.

3 Open a jump ring (Basics) and attach the 8mm-bead unit to the spacer unit. Close the jump ring. Use a jump ring to attach the dangle to the loop of an earring wire. Make a second earring to match the first.

Venture into the woods

Try different colors and textures for a range of looks

by Roxie Moede

Jazz up round wooden beads by selecting different stains and adding some carved options. Your choice of spacers can take this necklace and earrings from funky to formal.

1 **necklace •** Cut a piece of beading wire (Basics). (My necklaces are 22 in./56cm.) Center an alternating pattern of five spacers and four 20–22mm beads.

2 On each end, string: 16mm bead, spacer, 16mm, spacer, 16mm.

3 On each end, string an alternating pattern of spacers and 10mm beads until the strand is within 1½ in. (3.8cm) of the finished length.

4 On each end, string a spacer, two rondelles, a crimp bead, and half of the clasp. Check the fit, and add or remove beads if necessary. Go back through the last few beads strung and tighten the wire. Crimp the crimp bead (Basics) and trim the excess wire.

1 **earrings •** On a head pin, string a 6º seed bead, a 10mm bead, a rondelle, and a spacer. Make a wrapped loop (Basics).

2 Open the loop of an earring wire (Basics) and attach the dangle. Close the loop. Make a second earring to match the first.

DESIGN OPTIONS

Use fire-polished crystals or spacers in bright, contrasting colors to give wooden jewelry an entirely different feel.

Supply List

• chainnose or crimping pliers
• diagonal wire cutters

necklace
• **4** 20–22mm round wooden beads
• **6** 16mm round wooden beads
• **18–22** 10mm round wooden beads
• **4** 8mm wooden rondelles
• **29–33** 6–8mm spacers
• flexible beading wire, .014 or .015
• **2** crimp beads
• snap clasp

earrings
• **2** 10mm round wooden beads
• **2** 8mm wooden rondelles
• **2** 6º seed beads
• **2** 6–8mm spacers
• **2** 2-in. (5cm) head pins
• pair of earring wires
• chainnose and roundnose pliers
• diagonal wire cutters

Quick leaf bracelet

Larger accent beads make stringing easy

by Maureen Vallicelli

A simple pattern using large leaf-shaped beads comes together in a few minutes. To extend the motif without matching too much, try earrings in a similar shape but with different materials. I used glass beads in tortoise and black to match the bracelet colors and finish.

1 bracelet • Cut a piece of beading wire (Basics) and center a leaf-shaped bead.

2 On each end, string: 4mm round bead, rondelle, spacer, 6mm round bead, spacer, rondelle, 4mm, leaf. Repeat until the bracelet is within 1 in. (2.5cm) of the finished length.

3 On each end, string a spacer, a crimp bead, a spacer, and half of the clasp. Check the fit, and add or remove beads from each end if necessary. Go back through the beads just strung and tighten the wire. Crimp the crimp bead (Basics) and trim the excess wire.

Supply List

bracelet

- **3** 18–22mm Hill Tribes silver leaf-shaped beads
- **3–4** 6mm faceted round beads
- **7–8**mm faceted round beads
- **6–8** 3–4mm rondelles
- **10–12** 2–3mm spacers
- flexible beading wire, .014 or .015
- **2** crimp beads
- toggle clasp
- chainnose or crimping pliers
- diagonal wire cutters

earrings

- **2** 18–25mm triangular or leaf-shaped beads
- **2** 3–4mm rondelles
- **2** 2–3mm spacers
- **2** 2-in. (5cm) head pins
- pair of earring wires
- chainnose and roundnose pliers
- diagonal wire cutters

1 **earrings** • On a head pin, string a rondelle, a triangular or leaf-shaped bead, and a spacer. Make a wrapped loop (Basics).

2 Open the loop of an earring wire (Basics). Attach the dangle and close the loop. Make a second earring to match the first.

EDITOR'S TIP

For an asymmetrical bracelet, don't finish with the same pattern. Instead, string a shorter beaded pattern on one end.

Memory wire is great for short necklaces since it maintains its shape and doesn't need a clasp. Choose gemstones with clean lines, add definition with crystals, and perfect the geometric theme with round beads. You can add more rectangles, but stringing too many will cause the beads to flip up while you're wearing the necklace.

Around the block

String a quick, memory-wire necklace with gemstones in geometric shapes

by Naomi Fujimoto

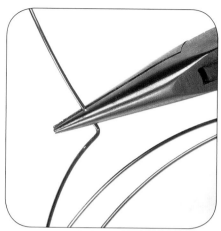

1 Wrap a coil of memory wire around your neck. Add 3 in. (7.6m), and cut the wire to that length with heavy-duty wire cutters. If you do not have heavy-duty wire cutters, grab the wire with chainnose pliers and bend it back and forth at one place until it breaks.

2 Alternate a crystal and a gemstone rectangle until you have strung the desired number of rectangles. End with a crystal.

3 String approximately 5½ in. (14cm) of round beads on each end. Tape the ends and check the fit. Add or remove beads if necessary. When the necklace is around your neck, the ends should overlap approximately 2 in. (5cm).

4 Remove the tape from one end. With roundnose pliers, turn a small loop. Cut or break the wire ½ in. (1.3cm) from the last bead on the other end, remove the tape, and turn a loop as before.

Supply List

- **8–12** 10 x 17mm top-drilled rectangular gemstones, mookite
- **16-in.** (41cm) strand 6mm round gemstones, mookite
- **9–13** 4mm bicone crystals
- **1** package necklace-diameter memory wire
- roundnose and chainnose pliers
- heavy-duty wire cutters (optional)

Seasonal beauty

Classic elements bring evergreen
style suitable for any season

by Rupa Balachander

Let this quick, classic
necklace accent your
wardrobe, whether it's spring,
fall, or in between.
The mother-of-pearl pendant,
framed by silver bamboo,
floats amid multicolored pearls.
Make simple pearl earrings,
and you're ready
for anything.

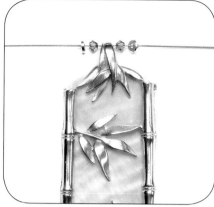

1 necklace • Cut a piece of beading wire (Basics). (My necklace is 17 in./43cm.) String: flat spacer, 3mm bicone crystal, pendant, 3mm bicone, flat spacer. Center the beads on the wire. The bail (pendant loop) should rest on top of the bicones.

2 On each end, string: pearl, flat spacer, 4mm bicone crystal, flat spacer. Repeat.

3 On each end, string five pearls, a flat spacer, a 4mm bicone, and a flat spacer. Repeat.

4 On each end, string pearls until the necklace is within 1 in. (2.5cm) of the finished length.

5 On each end, string a round spacer, a crimp bead, a round spacer, and half of a clasp. Check the fit, and add or remove beads from each end if necessary. Go back through the beads just strung and tighten the wire. Crimp the crimp bead (Basics) and trim the excess wire.

Supply List

necklace
- 25 x 55mm pendant
- 16-in. (41cm) strand 8mm round pearls
- **8** 4mm bicone crystals
- **2** 3mm bicone crystals
- **18** 3–4mm flat spacers
- **4** 3–4mm round spacers
- flexible beading wire, .014 or .015
- **2** crimp beads
- toggle clasp
- chainnose or crimping pliers
- diagonal wire cutters

earrings
- **2** 8mm round pearls
- **2** 3–4mm flat spacers
- **2** 3–4mm round or faceted spacers
- **2** 1½-in. (3.8cm) head pins
- pair of earring posts with ear nuts
- chainnose and roundnose pliers
- diagonal wire cutters

1 earrings • On a head pin, string a pearl, a flat spacer, and a round or faceted spacer. Make a plain loop (Basics).

2 Open the loop of an earring post (Basics). Attach the dangle and close the loop. Make a second earring to match the first.

EDITOR'S TIP

If you're making earrings, choose a pair of pearls before you string the necklace. I picked the sage-colored pearls because they match the pendant, but silver pearls would also have looked beautiful.

New York minute

Make a casual necklace in no time

by Lesa Shepherd and Cindi Swett

With a few beads and a few minutes, you can make a fun necklace that packs a fashion punch. A large-link chain lengthens the pendant, while a small link makes the look more compact. Vary the leather cord's length to suit your style — this necklace looks great as a choker or as a longer rope.

1 String three head pins with three chips, two head pins with an 8mm round, and one head pin with an 18mm bead and a rondelle. If the head pin slides through the 18mm bead's hole, add a spacer. Make the first half of a wrapped loop (Basics) above each bead.

2 Cut a 1½- to 2½-in. (3.8–6.4cm) length of chain. Slide the large bead unit's loop on the last link and complete the wraps.

Supply List

- 18mm round bead
- **9** gemstone chips
- **2** 8mm round beads
- 5mm faceted rondelle
- 6mm flat spacer (optional, depending on bead hole size)
- **6** 2-in. (5cm) decorative head pins
- 1½ to 2½ in. (3.8–6.4cm) cable chain, 4–6mm
- **2** crimp ends
- lobster claw clasp
- 6mm split ring
- 1½–2 ft. (46–61cm) 2mm leather cord
- chainnose and roundnose pliers
- diagonal wire cutters
- GS Hypo Cement

3 Attach one dangle to each link, alternating left and right sides. Complete the wraps as you go. Trim the chain if desired.

4 Determine the finished length of your necklace. (My blue necklace is 18 in./46cm; My coral necklace is 24 in./61cm.) Cut a piece of leather 1 in. (2.5cm) shorter than that length. String the top link of chain on the leather cord and center the pendant.

5 Attach a crimp end (Basics) to one end of the leather cord. Repeat on the other end. On one end, attach a split ring and a clasp.

Hammered-wire earrings

With textured silver wire and bicone crystals, these starburst earrings are made to dazzle. You'll see how hammering gives plain wire a fashion-forward finish.

Hammering creates a matte finish for these wire earrings

by Steven James

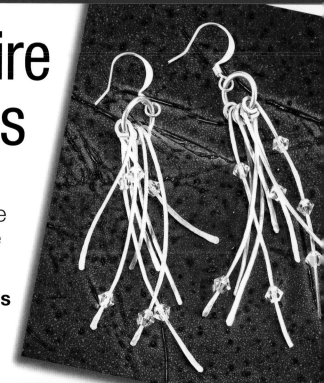

Supply List

- **12–16** 4mm bicone crystals
- 24–40 in. (61–102cm) 20-gauge half-hard wire
- 2 6–8mm inside diameter jump rings

- pair of earring wires
- chainnose and roundnose pliers
- diagonal wire cutters
- ball-peen hammer
- bench block or anvil
- metal file or emery board

EDITOR'S TIP

After stringing a crystal, move it off the edge of the bench block or anvil so the wire will lie flat against the work surface.

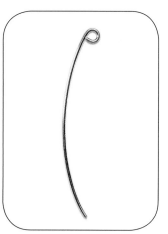

1 Cut eight 1½–2½-in. (3.8–6.4cm) pieces of wire. Curve each wire slightly. Using roundnose pliers, make a small loop on one end of each wire.

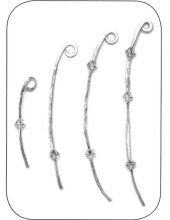

2 Place the loop end of a wire on a bench block or anvil, and hammer a small portion of it to add the desired texture. String a crystal and hammer the remaining wire. Repeat with three other wires, stringing one to three crystals and hammering sections of each wire.

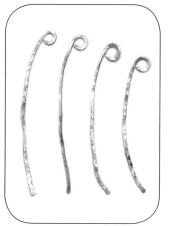

3 Place an unhammered wire on a bench block or anvil, and hammer it. Repeat with the remaining three wires.

4 If any of the wire loops opened during hammering, use roundnose pliers to close them. File any rough edges.

    Open a 6–8mm jump ring (Basics). Attach an earring wire and the hammered wires, positioning them so they curve in different directions. Close the jump ring. Make a second earring to match the first.

FASTEST

• under 15 minutes •

When you need a piece of jewelry right now — as a last-minute gift or to accessorize tonight's outfit — try a glass-bead necklace (page 72) or a wire ring (page 82). In just a few minutes, whip up a beaded neck wire (page 86) or chunky, wooden hoop earrings (page 70).

Jump through hoops the easy way

Accent wooden hoop earrings with beads and chain

by Naomi Fujimoto

Since wooden hoops are available in a wide array of colors and finishes, a lot of the design work is done for you. Here are three quick and easy earring designs you can practically make on your way out the door.

1 **double-hoop earrings** • On a head pin, string one hole of a small hoop and one hole of a large hoop. Make a wrapped loop (Basics).

2 Open the loop of an earring wire (Basics). Attach the dangle and close the loop. Make a second earring to match the first.

Supply List

double-hoop earrings
- **2** wooden hoops, approximately 50mm
- **2** wooden hoops, approximately 30mm
- **2** 2-in. (5cm) head pins
- pair of earring wires
- chainnose and roundnose pliers
- diagonal wire cutters

metallic hoop earrings
- **2** metallic wooden hoops, approximately 50mm

- **2** 8–12mm metal accent beads
- **2** 3–5mm spacers
- **2** 2-in. (5cm) head pins
- pair of earring wires
- chainnose and roundnose pliers
- diagonal wire cutters

hoop-and-chain earrings
- **2** wooden hoops, approximately 50mm
- 2½–4 in. (6.4–10cm) chain, 3–4mm links
- pair of earring posts with ear nuts
- chainnose pliers
- diagonal wire cutters

EDITOR'S TIP

If you want to use a longer chain for the hoop-and-chain earrings, try one with larger links. That way, the hoop and the chain will look balanced.

1 **metallic hoop earrings** • On a head pin, string one hole of a hoop, an accent bead, and a spacer. Make a plain loop (Basics).

2 Open the loop of an earring wire (Basics). Attach the dangle and close the loop. Make a second earring to match the first.

hoop-and-chain earrings • Cut a 1¼–2-in. (3.2–5cm) piece of chain. Center a hoop on the chain. Open the loop of an earring post (Basics). Attach each end of the chain and close the loop. Make a second earring to match the first.

Katherine Nesci, an instructor at the Sonoran Glass Art Academy (sonoranglass.org), creates these beads. String sets together for interchangeable centerpieces and you'll be fashion-ready in a flash.

Art interchange

Swap art beads for time-saving necklace options

by Katherine Nesci

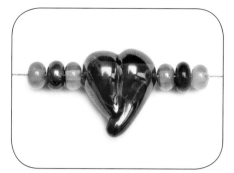

1 Cut a 7-in. (18cm) piece of beading wire. String three rondelles, a focal bead, and three rondelles. Center the beads on the wire.

2 On each end, string a spacer, a crimp bead, a spacer, and a hook clasp. Go back through the beads just strung and tighten the wire. Crimp the crimp bead (Basics) and trim the excess wire. Close a crimp cover over the crimp bead.

Supply List

- set of art-glass beads (20–30mm focal bead and 6 8–15mm rondelles from Glass Obsession, glassobsession.com)
- **2** 10mm crystals
- **8** 4mm spacers
- **4** 8mm bead caps
- flexible beading wire, .018 or .019
- 6 in. (15cm) 22-gauge half-hard wire
- 14–16 in. (36–41cm) chain, 2–4mm links
- **2** crimp beads
- **2** crimp covers
- **2** hook clasps
- chainnose and roundnose pliers
- diagonal wire cutters
- crimping pliers (optional)

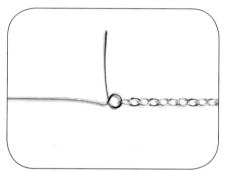

3 Decide how long you want your necklace to be. (My necklaces are 21 in./53cm.) Subtract 6 in. (15cm) and cut a piece of chain to that length.

Cut a 3-in. (7.6cm) piece of 22-gauge wire. Make the first half of a wrapped loop (Basics) and attach it to one end of the chain. Complete the wraps. Repeat on the remaining end.

4 On each wire, string: spacer, bead cap, crystal, bead cap, spacer. Make a wrapped loop.

EDITOR'S TIP

For security, make the wrapped loops just big enough to fit over the hook clasps.

5 To wear the centerpiece: Attach each hook clasp to a wrapped loop.

Cross promotion

String a bold pearl necklace and earrings in minutes

by Naomi Fujimoto

For an edgy necklace, string X-shaped pearls. When they're combined with crystals, the result is a lush, organic necklace. A pair of single-pearl earrings looks sharp.

Supply List

necklace
- 16-in. (41cm) strand 25–35mm X- or cross-shaped pearls
- **26–36** 6mm crystal rondelles
- flexible beading wire, .014 or .015
- **2** crimp beads
- toggle clasp
- chainnose or crimping pliers
- diagonal wire cutters

earrings
- **2** 25–35mm X- or cross-shaped pearls left over from necklace
- **2** 2-in. (5cm) head pins
- pair of earring wires
- chainnose and roundnose pliers
- diagonal wire cutters

1 **necklace** • Cut a piece of beading wire (Basics). (My necklace is 19 in./48cm.) Center a pearl on the wire.

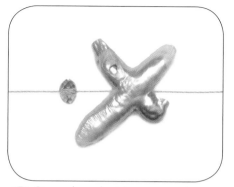

2 On each end, string a crystal rondelle and a pearl. Repeat until the strand is within 1 in. (2.5cm) of the finished length, ending with a pearl.

3 On each end, string a rondelle, a crimp bead, a rondelle, and half of the clasp. Check the fit, and add or remove beads from each end if necessary. Go back through the beads just strung and tighten the wire. Crimp the crimp bead (Basics) and trim the excess wire.

EDITOR'S TIP

If you're making earrings, select two pearls before you make the necklace. Because the pearls are irregularly shaped, they won't match, but choose two that are about the same size.

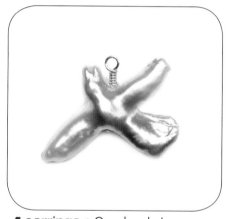

1 **earrings** • On a head pin, string a pearl. Make a wrapped loop (Basics).

2 Open the loop of an earring wire (Basics). Attach the bead unit and close the loop. Make a second earring to match the first.

DESIGN OPTION

I used Swarovski crystal rondelles in vintage rose between the X-shaped pearls. If you like, try using smaller crystals, round pearls, and/or gold spacers instead.

To make casual bracelets, position a few color-coordinated beads on silver wire. Because you can make them economically and quickly, you may want to string one for each day of the week.

Take the bracelet express

Colorful beads drive a wristful of sporty bracelets

by Andrea Loss

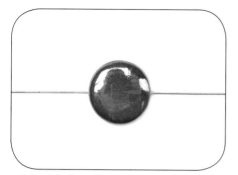

1 Decide how long you want your bracelet to be. Double that measurement, add 3 in. (7.6cm), and cut a piece of beading wire to that length. Center a focal bead on the wire.

2 On each end, string: spacer, accent bead, spacer, accent bead, two crimp beads.

Supply List

- 12–20mm focal bead
- **4** 4–10mm accent beads
- **4** 4mm spacers
- flexible beading wire, .014 or .015
- **4** crimp beads
- lobster claw clasp and soldered jump ring
- chainnose or crimping pliers
- diagonal wire cutters

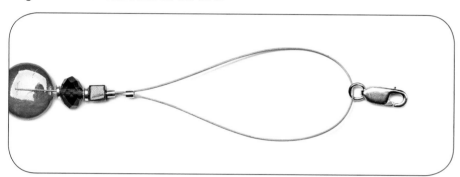

3 On one end, string a lobster claw clasp. Go back through the beads just strung. Repeat on the other end, substituting a soldered jump ring for the clasp.

EDITOR'S TIP

Flexible beading wire is available in a variety of colors. Choose one to complement the color of the focal bead.

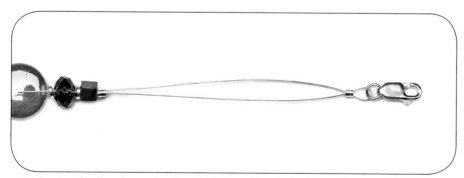

4 Center the beads on the doubled wire. Check the fit, and adjust the wire if necessary. On each side, crimp one crimp bead (Basics) next to the centered section of beads. Trim the excess wire, hiding the end in the focal bead. Slide each remaining crimp bead out to the end, and crimp it.

Capture
a golden glow

Necklace, bracelet, and earrings catch the light

by Cathy Jakicic

Frosted glass beads seem lit from within. Accent them simply with beads and rondelles that reflect their subtle shimmer in this quick trio.

1 necklace • Cut a piece of beading wire (Basics). (My necklace is 15 in./38cm.) On the wire, center: rhinestone rondelle, 7mm bead, rondelle, round bead, rondelle, 7mm, rondelle.

2 On each end, string a round and a 7mm. Repeat until the strand is within 1 in. (2.5cm) of the finished length.

3 On one end, string a 7mm, a crimp bead, and a lobster claw clasp. Repeat on the other end, substituting a soldered jump ring for the clasp. Check the fit, and add or remove beads if necessary. Go back through the last few beads strung and tighten the wire. Crimp the crimp bead (Basics) and trim the excess wire.

1 **bracelet** • Cut a piece of beading wire (Basics). On the wire, string a round bead and a 6mm rondelle. Repeat until the strand is within ½ in. (1.3cm) of the finished length.

2 On each end, string a crimp bead and half of the clasp. Check the fit, and add or remove beads if necessary. Go back through the last few beads strung and tighten the wire. Crimp the crimp bead (Basics) and trim the excess wire.

1 **earrings** • On a head pin, string a 6mm rondelle, a rhinestone rondelle, and a 7mm bead. Make a wrapped loop (Basics).

2 Open the loop of an earring wire (Basics). Attach the dangle and close the loop. Make a second earring to match the first.

Supply List

necklace
- 12-in. (30cm) strand 10mm round glass beads
- **4** 8mm rhinestone rondelles
- 6-in. (15cm) strand 7mm beads
- flexible beading wire, .014 or .015
- **2** crimp beads
- lobster claw clasp and soldered jump ring
- chainnose or crimping pliers
- diagonal wire cutters

bracelet
- **10** 10mm round glass beads
- 6-in. (15cm) strand 6mm rondelles
- flexible beading wire, .014 or .015
- **2** crimp beads
- snap clasp
- chainnose or crimping pliers
- diagonal wire cutters

earrings
- **2** 8mm rhinestone rondelles
- **2** 7mm beads
- **2** 6mm rondelles
- **2** 2-in. (5cm) head pins
- pair of earring wires
- chainnose and roundnose pliers
- diagonal wire cutters

DESIGN OPTION
Take advantage of leftover beads to make a second earring option.

In less than 15 minutes, you can make two pairs of contemporary earrings. Try teardrop-shaped hoops (make a few pairs in different sizes). Or whip up hook earrings with a striking column of beads.

Expedite your earrings

With a quick turn of wire, get instant earrings

by Christine Haynes

1 hoop earrings • Cut a 3–5-in. (7.6–13cm) piece of wire. Wrap it around a pill bottle, 35mm-film canister, or other round object to make a drop shape. String six or seven rondelles.

2 On each end, use roundnose pliers to make a loop.

3 To harden the wire, hammer it gently on a bench block or anvil. Turn the wire over and hammer the other side.

4 Open the loop of an earring wire (Basics). Attach each wire loop and close the loop of the earring wire. Make a second earring to match the first.

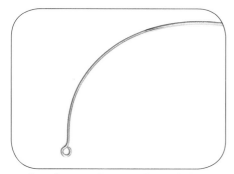

1 **hook earrings** • Cut a 4–5-in. (10–13cm) piece of wire. Make a plain loop (Basics) on one end.

2 String four beads. At the wire's halfway point, bend it around a pen barrel.

3 To harden the wire, hammer it gently at the bend on a bench block or anvil. Turn the wire over and hammer the other side. File the end if necessary. Make a second earring to match the first.

EDITOR'S TIP

Use 24-gauge wire if you're stringing small-hole beads like pearls. Because the wire is more pliable than 20- or 22-gauge wire, make sure to hammer it after adding the beads. That way, the earring will maintain its shape.

Supply List

hoop earrings
- **12** or **14** 10–12mm rondelles
- 6–10 in. (15–25cm) 20- or 22-gauge half-hard wire
- pair of earring wires
- chainnose and roundnose pliers
- diagonal wire cutters
- bench block or anvil (optional)
- hammer (optional)

hook earrings
- **8** 6–10mm beads
- 8–10 in. (20–25cm) 20- or 22-gauge half-hard wire
- chainnose and roundnose pliers
- diagonal wire cutters
- bench block or anvil (optional)
- hammer (optional)
- metal file or emery board (optional)

A passion for poppies

Wrap fresh flower rings

by Jane Konkel

Nanette Young-Greiner's lampworked flower beads are ideal for rings, since heavy-gauge wire fits easily through the large center hole. For a colorful bouquet, try wearing a bunch of these blossoms on one finger.

1 Cut a 15-in. (38cm) piece of wire. Make a right-angle bend ¾ in. (1.9cm) from one end.
 With the tip of your roundnose pliers, grasp the short wire at the bend. Wrap the short wire around the pliers to form a small coil.

2 String a flower bead on the wire. Make a right-angle bend under the flower.

3 Locate your ring size on a ring mandrel. Wrap the remaining end of the wire around the mandrel, one size smaller than your actual ring size.

4 Wrap the tail around the stem between the ring band and the flower. Trim the excess wire.

EDITOR'S TIP

To find your ring size, wrap a strip of paper around your finger, tape the paper, and slip it onto a ring mandrel.

Supply List

- 25mm lampworked flower bead
- 15 in. (38cm) 18-gauge dead-soft wire
- roundnose pliers
- diagonal wire cutters
- ring mandrel

Showcase a simple pendant

Gemstones and silver harmonize with nature

by Lindsay Mikulsky

An engraved silver pendant looks beautiful with a basic setting of gemstones and faceted spacers. Pastel-hued aquamarine is nicely refreshing, or the neutral tones of blue tigereye make a stronger statement.

EDITOR'S TIP

A round magnetic clasp is a great choice for these necklaces. The shape mimics the round gemstones, and the necklace's light weight guarantees that the clasp will stay fastened. Clasps are available from Artbeads.com, (866) 715-2323.

1 Cut a piece of beading wire (Basics). (My necklaces are 15 in./38cm.) Center a pendant on the wire.

2 On each end, string a 4mm round bead and a 2mm faceted spacer. Repeat until the necklace is within 1 in. (2.5cm) of the finished length.

Supply List

- 20mm Thai-silver pendant (Artbeads.com, 866-715-2323)
- 16-in. (41cm) strand 4mm round gemstone beads
- 4 3mm round silver spacers
- 30–40 2mm faceted Thai-silver spacers (Artbeads.com)
- flexible beading wire, .014 or .015
- 2 crimp beads
- magnetic clasp
- chainnose or crimping pliers
- diagonal wire cutters

3 On each end, string a 3mm round spacer, a crimp bead, a 3mm round spacer, and half of the clasp. Check the fit, and add or remove beads from each end if necessary. Go back through the beads just strung and tighten the wire. Crimp the crimp bead (Basics) and trim the excess wire.

Simplify stringing with premixed assortments of seed bead on hanks and run your beading wire through individual strands. Or blend your own mix with different amounts of seed bead colors. Keep the delicate look of the seed beads in mind when selecting your accent beads.

Sowing the seeds

String seed beads with a few gemstone chips and add a clasp

by Naomi Fujimoto

1 Cut a piece of beading wire (Basics). (The gemstone chip necklaces are 15 in./38cm; the yellow jasper necklace, 16 in./41cm.). Center an accent bead on the wire. If you're using several accent beads, string a few seed beads between them.

2 Using the end of the beading wire to pick up beads, string assorted seed beads on each end until you are within 1 in. (2.5cm) of the desired length.

3 String a crimp bead, a seed bead, and the clasp. Go back through the beads just strung and tighten the wire. Repeat on the other end, substituting a soldered jump ring for the clasp. Check the fit, and add or remove beads from each end if necessary. Crimp the crimp beads (Basics) and trim the excess wire.

Supply List

- 5g size 11º seed beads, assorted colors
- assorted gemstone chips or accent beads
- flexible beading wire, .014 or .015
- **2** crimp beads
- lobster claw clasp and soldered jump ring
- chainnose or crimping pliers
- diagonal wire cutters

No tools necessary

A scalloped necklace wire is the first step toward endless stringing options

by Cathy Jakicic

Most of the time you spend on this necklace will be devoted to deciding which fashionable option to make. After that, the necklace comes together in no time — with no tools!

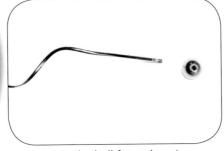

1 Unscrew the ball from the wire.

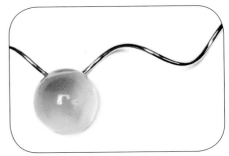

2 String ten to 14 beads on the wire. Apply glue to the end and screw the ball on.

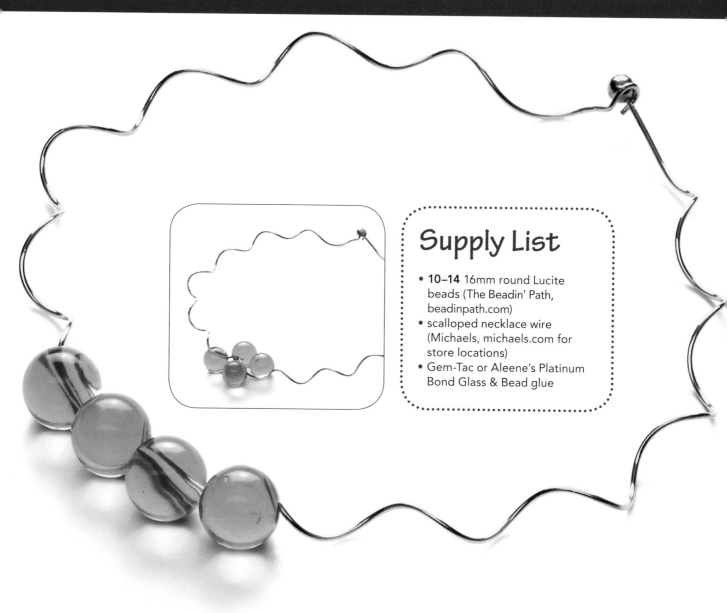

Supply List

- **10–14** 16mm round Lucite beads (The Beadin' Path, beadinpath.com)
- scalloped necklace wire (Michaels, michaels.com for store locations)
- Gem-Tac or Aleene's Platinum Bond Glass & Bead glue

DESIGN OPTIONS

• String large-hole metal spacers that will flow with the curves.

• To show more of the wire's shape, string fewer Lucite beads (above).
• String a single, striking pendant, such as a crystal.

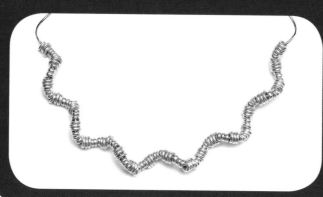

Big beads, crystals, and a few minutes are all you need to make a bracelet with timeless appeal. Rectangular beads are available in a variety of gemstones, including tigereye and chalcedony, so you'll have an excuse to make more than one.

String a classic bracelet in a snap

Large rectangular beads are a stylish shortcut to quick and easy jewelry

by Eva Kapitany

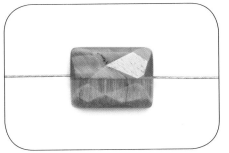

1 Cut a piece of beading wire (Basics). Center a rectangular bead on the wire.

2 On each end, string three spacers, a crystal, three spacers, and a rectangular bead. Repeat until the bracelet is within 1 in. (2.5cm) of the finished length. End with three spacers.

3 On each end, string a crimp bead, a spacer, and half of the clasp. Check the fit, and add or remove beads from each end if necessary. Go back through the last few beads strung and tighten the wire. Crimp the crimp bead (Basics) and trim the excess wire.

Supply List

- **4–5** 14–16mm rectangular gemstone beads
- **5–6** 8mm round crystals
- **32–38** 4–5mm flat spacers
- flexible beading wire, .014 or .015
- **2** crimp beads
- toggle clasp
- chainnose or crimping pliers
- diagonal wire cutters

WHERE TO SHOP

14mm rectangular beads are available from Rings & Things, rings-things.com.
16mm rectangular beads are available from Eclectica, (262) 641-0910.

EDITOR'S TIP

Five rectangular beads make a 7½–8-in. (19.1–20cm) bracelet. Four rectangular beads make a 6–6½-in. (15–16.5cm) bracelet.

String kite-shaped beads for style on the fly

A necklace of kite-shaped beads makes for high fashion

by Rupa Balachandar

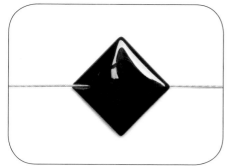

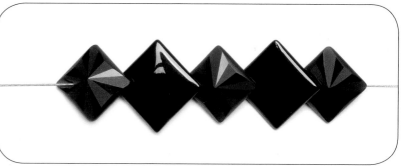

1 Cut a piece of beading wire (Basics). (My necklace is 18½ in./47cm.) Center an 18mm kite-shaped bead on the wire.

2 On each end, string: 16mm kite-shaped bead, 18mm, 16mm, 18mm, 16mm. String 18mms until the strand is within 1 in. (2.5cm) of the finished length.

3 On each end, string: spacer, crystal, spacer, crimp bead, Wire Guardian, half of a clasp. Check the fit, and add or remove beads from each end if necessary. Go back through the beads just strung and tighten the wire. Crimp the crimp bead (Basics), and trim the excess wire.

Supply List

- 16-in. (41cm) strand 18mm overlapping kite-shaped beads (Rupa B. Designs, rupab.com)
- **6** 16mm laser-cut overlapping kite-shaped beads
- **2** 5mm bicone crystals
- **4** 3mm flat spacers
- flexible beading wire, .014 or .015
- **2** crimp beads
- **2** Wire Guardians
- box clasp
- chainnose or crimping pliers
- diagonal wire cutters

Look sharp in a quick, simple necklace that uses overlapping kite-shaped beads. Angular beads look edgy, but the monochromatic color scheme is classic.

Lending an earring

String a quick, elegant necklace with an earring as a pendant

by Beth Stone

Showcase an antique or vintage earring on a strand of freshwater pearls. Whether the earring is an heirloom or was a lucky estate-sale find, it adds a touch of glamour to a tried-and-true classic. If your earring is part of a pair, make a second necklace to share.

1 Cut a piece of beading wire (Basics). (My necklaces are 17½ in./44.5cm.) Open a jump ring (Basics) and attach the earring. Close the jump ring and center the earring on the wire.

2 On each end, string pearls until the necklace is within 1½ in. (3.8cm) of the desired length.

3 On one end, string: flat spacer, round spacer, crimp bead, round spacer, one loop of the connector. Go back through the beads just strung and tighten the wire. Repeat on the other end, substituting a clasp for the connector. Check the fit, and add or remove pearls from each end if necessary. Crimp the crimp beads (Basics) and trim the excess wire.

DESIGN OPTIONS

• Earring posts and clip-on hinges can prevent the earring from lying flat. Trim excess metal from the back of the earring with heavy-duty wire cutters, and file any rough edges.
• Not all earrings will require the use of a jump ring. If an earring has a perpendicular loop at the top, you can omit the jump ring.
• If genuine antiques are not available, consider antique-inspired earrings (available at 1928 Jewelry, 1928.com).

Supply List

• antique or vintage earring
• 16-in. (41cm) strand 4–5mm pearls
• **2** 5mm flat spacers
• **4** 4mm round spacers
• flexible beading wire, .014 or .015
• 3–4mm jump ring (optional)
• **2** crimp beads
• spring-ring or lobster claw clasp and 9–13mm connector
• chainnose and roundnose pliers
• diagonal wire cutters
• crimping pliers (optional)

Both cultivated and casual, leather necklaces are everywhere. Make your version with marcasite beads that lend an Art Deco sparkle and have large holes for stringing. The faceted pearl and neutral colors make this necklace a natural for any outfit — minimal effort for maximum impact.

Pretty practical

Merge contemporary and classic styles in a casual necklace

by Irina Miech

1 String a pearl on a head pin. Make the first half of a wrapped loop (Basics). Slide the loop into the bail's bottom loop. Complete the wraps.

2 Determine the finished length of your necklace (mine is 18 in./46cm) and cut a piece of leather cord to this length. Center the bail on the leather.

3 On each side of the bail, string a marcasite spacer, a large-hole spacer, and a marcasite tube.

4 Check the fit. To shorten the necklace, cut off leather from one of the ends. Attach a crimp end on one end (Basics). Repeat on the other end.

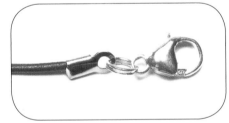

5 Attach a split ring (Basics) to the each crimp end. Attach half the toggle clasp to each split ring, or attach a lobster claw clasp to one split ring.

Supply List

- **2** 3 x 7mm marcasite spacers
- **2** 5 x 10mm marcasite tubes
- **2** 5 x 7mm large-hole spacers
- faceted pearl, approx. 8 x 11mm
- bail, approx. 6 x 10mm
- **2** ft. (61cm) 1mm-diameter round leather cord
- **2** crimp ends
- **2** split rings
- 1½-in. (3.8cm) head pin
- toggle or lobster claw clasp
- E6000 glue
- chainnose and roundnose pliers
- diagonal wire cutters
- split-ring pliers (optional)

CONTRIBUTORS

Contact **Stephanie Baker** at bluedamselflyjewelry@yahoo.com.

Rupa Balachandar's jewelry makes a strong statement. She regularly travels Asia looking for unusual elements and is pleased to share her finds through her Web site, rupab.com. Contact Rupa at info@rupab.com

Naomi Fujimoto is senior editor of *BeadStyle* magazine and author of *Cool Jewels: Beading Projects for Teens*. Visit her blog at cooljewelsnaomi.blogspot.com, or contact her at nfujimoto@kalmbach.com.

Contact **Christine Haynes** via e-mail at jewelry@fezelry.com, or visit her Web site at fezelry.com.

Catherine Hodge designs jewelry focused on beauty and balance. She began by creating for herself and now designs "perfect find" pieces for others. Contact Catherine via e-mail at catherinemarissa@yahoo.com, or her Web site, catherinemarissa.com.

Cathy Jakicic is editor of *BeadStyle* and author of *Hip Handmade Memory Jewelry*. Contact Cathy at Cjakicic@kalmbach.com.

Armed with his mantra, "What are you gonna make today?," **Steven James** incorporates beads and jewelry making into home décor and everyday living. Visit his Web site, macaroniandglitter.com.

Eva Kapitany began making jewelry when, instead of prescribing medication, her doctor suggested she find a fun activity to ease her depression. Eva's been depression-free and designing jewelry for seven years. Contact Eva in care of *BeadStyle*.

Jane Konkel, associate editor of *BeadStyle*, can be reached at jkonkel@kalmbach.com.

Contact **Andrea Loss** at amloss@wi.rr.com.

Carol McKinney calls on her interior design expertise to enhance her jewelry designs. Contact Carol at lemon.leopard@hotmail.com or visit lemonleopard.com.

Irina Miech is a teacher, artist, and the author of *Metal Clay for Beaders, More Metal Clay for Beaders, Inventive Metal Clay,* and *Beautiful Wire Jewelry for Beaders*. Her newest title, *Metal Clay Rings,* will be released in early 2010.

Former Editorial Associate of *BeadStyle* **Lindsay Mikulsky** is currently pursuing a career in education. Contact her at lindsayrose5@gmail.com.

Contact **Roxie Moede** at rmoede@kalmbach.com.

Katherine Nesci draws inspiration from the desert flowers outside her Tuscon, Ariz., home. Contact Katherine via e-mail at knesci@aol.com, or visit her Web site, glassobsession.com.

Contact **Cari Rosen** via e-mail at rosenwv@mac.com, or visit her Web site pixiedustdesignsjewelry.com to see her work.

Lesa Shepherd and **Cindi Swett** are the co-founders of Bead Retreat Ltd., a home-party beading business. Contact them at info@beadretreat.com, (888) 708-2323 or visit beadretreat.com.

Debbi Simon paints, teaches, and designs and makes jewelry. She is the author of *Crystal Chic: Custom Jewelry with Dazzling Details*.

Beth Stone is the author of *Seed Bead Stitching: Creative Variations on Traditional Techniques*. Contact her via e-mail at bnshdl@msn.com, or visit her Web site, beth-stone.com. Look for her upcoming book, *More Seed Bead Stitching,* later this year.

Contact **Maureen Vallicelli** in care of Kalmbach Books.

Wendy Witchner is a wire and metal jewelry artist who travels the United States in her motor home to sell her creations at art shows. Her work is also available at select galleries. Visit her Web site, wendywitchner-jewelry.com.

Easy beaded jewelry inspired by cut, color

and the calendar

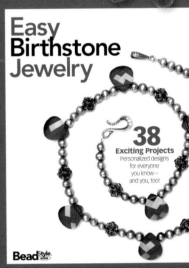

JEWELRY JUST FOR YOU!

Projects that flatter every face shape and neckline

round face **heart-shaped face** oval face square
eck strapless round neckline turtleneck v-neck

Jewelry Just for You! gives you 32 projects divided into either face shape or neckline, with step-by-step photo instructions for a necklace and a pair of earrings that go well with your face and what you're wearing.
62618 • $19.95

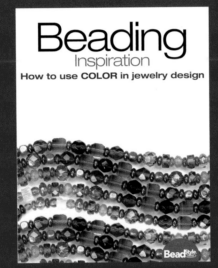

Beading
Inspiration
How to use COLOR in jewelry design

Beading Inspiration explores using nature, the color wheel, decorative art, and fabric for color inspiration in 16 projects from the pages of *Beading Basics: Color*, plus six all-new designs.
62465 • $19.95

Easy Birthstone Jewelry

38 Exciting Projects
Personalized designs for everyone you know – and you, too!

Easy Birthstone Jewelry features 37 beautiful birthstone projects with step-by-step instructions, gemstone choices— traditional or alternate, and a few basic techniques.
62557 • $21.95